Other Books by the Author

When The Wind Blows

A Memoir

Elaine Beachy

WESTBOW
PRESS®
A DIVISION OF THOMAS NELSON
& ZONDERVAN

WestBow Press books may be ordered through booksellers or by contacting:

WestBow Press
A Division of Thomas Nelson & Zondervan
1663 Liberty Drive
Bloomington, IN 47403
www.westbowpress.com
844-714-3454

ISBN: 978-1-6642-4875-5 (sc)
ISBN: 978-1-6642-4874-8 (e)

Print information available on the last page.

WestBow Press rev. date: 11/08/2021

Dedication

To my dear family—my children, their spouses, my grandchildren, and future family members. I want you to know my spiritual journey with the hope that it will bless and enhance your own spiritual walk. Please know I pray for you daily—even those yet unborn.

May you experience the wind of the Holy Spirit in your own lives, and always keep Jesus as your first love. Live in the freedom of the Holy Spirit. Don't live by worldly wisdom, but rather "Trust in the Lord with all your heart and lean not on your own understanding; in all your ways acknowledge Him, and He shall direct your paths" (Proverbs 3:5 – 6).

My desire is to honor God with my life. May His kingdom come, and His will be done on earth, as it is in heaven. Keep us all in Your truth.

Contents

Preface

No, *When the Wind Blows* is not a reference to that dismal nursery rhyme, *Rock-A-Bye-Baby*. Rather, it refers to the wind of the Holy Spirit as He blew across my life of seventy-five years thus far. How did a Mennonite girl, born of Amish parents, become a Charismatic?

Although this book is somewhat like an autobiography, it is a memoir in that I specifically show the Holy Spirit at work throughout my life. My dear family and friends, I hope that you too will recognize and experience the wind of the Holy Spirit upon your own lives.

As I finished writing this memoir, and then proof-read it umpteen times, I suddenly realized that, mixed in with all the good things in my life, I had experienced a lot of rejection, had craved acceptance and approval.

Life and relationships can be painful at times, but I am so glad that my love for others far outweighs any feelings of rejection anyone may have caused me. I hold no ill feelings toward anyone and have forgiven all who caused pain in my life. We all have our faults and failures, especially yours truly. And there is victory and healing for every emotional wound, as I show in the following example.

On my refrigerator I have a laminated copy of Psalm 91, and pretty much have it memorized. Several years ago, someone in a church made remarks that deeply hurt me one Sunday, so much so that I could hardly eat my lunch after we got home.

In my heart, I prayed, "God, please help me with this pain; take it from me."

I happened to look up from my lunch plate and saw Psalm 91 on the fridge and instantly I recalled the phrase about the Lord delivering us from "the arrow that flies by day." Those words leaped within my spirit, and I received it as God's word to me. The arrows were those hurtful words. All the pain left, and peace came. It was truly miraculous! I didn't even remember anymore what was said that hurt me. The arrow was gone.

The names, dates and experiences in this book are true, based on the best of my ability to recall them. I pray my life will be a blessing to you.

———————

Chapter 1

The long, lazy, and hazy summer Sunday afternoon stretched out in emptiness before me as my twelve-year-old mind considered how to spend it. I often wished I had a sister to pal around with, and at times I envied my brothers who enjoyed one another's fun and companionship. Granted, there were times we all played board games like Uncle Wiggly, did a paint-by-number kit or worked on a puzzle together, but this Sunday, each had gone their separate ways. Mom, Dad, and baby brother George were napping, and I was alone.

I left the dining room and went onto our large front porch of the farmhouse where we lived near the town of Meyersdale, Pennsylvania. The coolness of the deep green leafy trees in the woods down over the hill beyond the lane that fronted our house, seemed to beckon me. I loved our Valley Brook Farm, so named by my paternal grandfather, Claude Yoder.

The afternoon was quite warm and wind-still as I picked my way carefully down the steep terrain, past the spring where it was rumored my great-grandmother Dora Yoder had hidden gold. *Would we ever find it? We could be rich!* I dismissed the thought and continued down to the safety of the bottom. The Quaking Aspen, whose leaves shimmered with silver and quivered with the slightest breeze, was my favorite tree. The gurgling sound of the brook greeted me as it meandered past the Aspen; its visible roots reaching out to drink deeply of the cool, refreshing water.

I turned left on this side of the brook at the shimmering silver tree, and my heart somehow drew me to a fallen log under a small group of trees deeper in the coolness of the woods. I sensed the stillness and special feeling of God's presence as I carefully positioned my skirt under me and sat down there, alone with Him. My heart filled with love and thanksgiving for my newly found Savior.

The buzzing sounds of copious insects accompanied my thoughts.

Only a year earlier, I had stood to my feet in a revival meeting at First Mennonite Church to publicly declare that I was a Christian. I had privately received Jesus as my Savior one Sunday morning in our living room as I listened to the Radio Kids Bible Class with J. C. Brumfield while the rest of my family was still upstairs getting ready for church. I saw my need for Jesus as the program unfolded, and I prayed to receive Him as my Savior at the end of the broadcast. But I told no one.

I thought of how I walked one day with my grandmother Olive down the lane from her house to ours. She had looked at me and asked, "You have become a Christian, haven't you?"

I answered, "Yes, I did." But I held back the question I wanted to ask her: *How could you tell?* I had not told anyone, and that was the way it stayed until one evening at revival meeting in our church.

I remembered how my heart had pounded in my chest and neck as I fought to gather courage to stand as the invitation was given to receive Jesus as Savior. I didn't want to feel conspicuous.

I'm not receiving Jesus; I already did that. . . But I didn't tell anyone. Maybe I should stand and let everyone know what I did. . . But do I really need to?

The tug of war continued until I suddenly found myself standing to my feet, and as I did, tears coursed down my face as I continued standing. Embarrassment at public confession was erased from my thoughts and relief washed over me. Boldness came into me. *I will not be ashamed of Jesus or be ashamed to let others know He is my Savior!*

After several weeks of instruction, as it was called, I had been water-baptized by the method of pouring in our Mennonite church. I knelt in front of the church, and the pastor was offered a basin of water. He cupped his hands into the water, and then poured it over my bowed head, saying, "Upon your confession of faith in the Lord Jesus Christ, I now baptize you in the name of the Father, the Son, and the Holy Spirit."

Pastor offered me his hand (I think it was Ressley Tressler) and said, "Rise, to walk in newness of life!" I did.

I remembered how, later at home, I hugged my Bible and kissed it, and whispered love things to Jesus. I admired my mother's devotion to the Word, and noticed she had many passages underlined in red in her Bible, so I found a red colored pencil and proceeded to underline the same verses in mine. I loved to read my Bible, even if some of the things in the King James version were sometimes hard to understand.

As I sat there in the woods in communion with God that Sunday afternoon, I prayed, "God, I want to always love the truth. Keep me in a love of the truth."

I also felt a deep emotional longing in my heart as I said to the Lord, "Oh, if only the miracles I read about in the New Testament still happened today! How I wish they were still true!"

I believed miracles and healing passed away when the last of Jesus's twelve disciples died, because that's what I heard explained to me. I couldn't recall anyone praying for healing in our Mennonite church, or at home. My eyes filled with tears as I expressed my longing to Jesus. *Why did healing and miracles have to pass away?*

I bowed my head and prayed.

On that log as I prayed that Sunday afternoon, I had a deep desire to utter strange-sounding words to God. So, in childlike faith, I did. I stayed and prayed there quite a while and enjoyed how special God felt to me. No one had ever taught me about being baptized by the Holy Spirit with the evidence of speaking in tongues, and I didn't even know such a thing existed. But I know now that is exactly what I experienced that day. I found something much better than great-grandmother Dora's gold! I wanted to write down the strange-sounding words, so I made the trek back up the steep hill to the farmhouse.

On the dresser in my bedroom, I had a wooden trinket box that contained small, blank pieces of smooth wood about one-eighth inch thick, two and a half inches long, and about three-quarter inch wide. I found a pencil and wrote down, phonetically, the numerous words I remembered I had uttered, and put them back in the box. I said to myself, "Those words sure sound Indian to me!" I never told anyone about the special strange experience I had that Sunday afternoon, but there is no doubt in my mind that the wind of the Holy Spirit had blown across my young life that day. And I know God heard the cry of my heart. Little did I know how the wind of the Spirit would continue to blow throughout my life.

Chapter 2

I was born September 6, 1946, in McMinnville, Oregon, to my parents, Edwin and Elva Yoder who were still more or less Amish. How does a girl, who grew up in Pennsylvania and Virginia on the eastern part of the United States, happen to have been born on the west coast? And how does a girl, whose parents were Amish, happen to end up a Charismatic?

My parents, Edwin and Elva Yoder, were born in Pennsylvania and I loved to hear their stories of Amish life as I grew up.

Mom said, "Daddy was always a sharp dresser and a bit of a rebel in the Amish church. He tied a decorative fox tail to his car antenna (they could have cars—but were forbidden to play the radio). However, based on the spirit of gaiety Mom and Dad displayed when they told the story, I could easily imagine he played the radio too when he could get away with it.

"He was 'called on the carpet' by the Amish bishops who said his socks needed to be solid in color—not striped," Mom continued. Daddy answered, 'Each stripe is one color!' "He truly was not Amish at heart, and I was glad about it. That's not to say the Amish aren't good people, but it's been my observation that far too many place their hope of eternal salvation on keeping the church rules, or the 'church letter.' To be submissive and obey the leaders or be shunned."

Mom and Dad were married in Pennsylvania and soon moved to Oregon to be with Mom's parents, Sam and Lydia Beachy. That's where I was born. My maternal grandparents and Auntie Fannie had moved there after Grandpa Sam and Lydia were reunited after many years of a painful separation—a separation that was totally unheard of in the Amish church.

As a young girl, I was incredulous when I found that out. "Mom, how was it even possible for a separation in marriage to happen, especially when they were in the Amish church?" I asked.

Mom said, "My parents married young (as I recall, she said Lydia was only sixteen and Sam was nineteen), lived on a farm, and had four children in the space of four years. My dad was deeply in debt. I suppose the strain of marriage, family life, and other factors were just too great for him, so he abandoned our family and moved out west to his sister and other family members.

"As a result, my mom and her siblings were sent to live with different relatives to earn their keep at a very young age. Mom's maternal grandfather paid off the debts Grandpa Sam had incurred that remained after a sale was made to sell off all household goods."

Mom said, "We only saw our mother on every other Sunday when there was church, and rarely on other occasions, because she had to find work. And the only work there was to be had was as a maid caring for other people's homes and children. Such was the Amish way. My mom's parents raised us children until we were sent to the homes of other relatives to work to earn our keep. I was only eight years old when I was sent away. It was extremely hard for me, and I had two tries at being separated from my grandparents until I was finally able to stick it out at age nine.

"I prayed and prayed for my dad to come home," Mom said. "My mom also kept praying and believing he would return one day. Many years passed. When I was about eighteen years old, I wrote my dad a letter and asked him to come home. Then one day, out of the blue, fourteen years after he'd abandoned our family, my dad walked across the front porch of our house where my mom was staying and was home! What a reunion of great joy and celebration followed as our family was reunited!"

I am sure there needed to be a lot of forgiveness all around, but nevertheless, the family was so glad he had come home. Mom told me that Grandpa Sam later said the Lord had visited him one night. He heard his children crying, and knew he had to go home, but he left behind a good job in Oregon, where he'd become quite prosperous.

The Amish church Sam and Lydia had attended refused to take him back into their fellowship. He was shunned, which meant nobody in the church could do business with him or even eat at the same table with him. But that's an extremely painful story—one that I'm not qualified to write. And you know what? I'm glad the result of that story was that Springs Mennonite Church welcomed Grandpa Sam warmly, and eventually Lydia joined him there. It was a wind of change that God used to deliver the family line from bondage to Amish rules and regulations that had no spiritual life in them. Who knows? Had Sam been allowed to stay in the Old Order Amish church fellowship, perhaps I would be Amish to this day. Perish the thought!

My dad found a good-paying job in Oregon, but after a while, my parents missed their families in Pennsylvania, so they decided to go back home when I was a year old, and my baby brother Stanley was three months old.

My dad's parents, Claude, and Olive Yoder invited our little family to stay with them until Dad could find work and a place for us to live, for we had arrived in Pennsylvania in November when jobs were scarce. My dad helped my Grandpa Claude with the farm work for a while, and when I was about three years old, the winds of change blew again, and we moved—to Virginia this time—so Dad could work for Will Overholt, a farmer in the Norfolk area. We lived in his tenant house.

That little tenant house with white clapboard siding and green window trim holds a lot of memories for me. We had an electric stove, but also had an old-fashioned cast iron cookstove that was rarely used. We probably burned wood in it to help heat the house in winter, because the house sat on concrete blocks and had no basement. Mom had to carry water to fill her wringer washer on the porch, and my parents also carried water to heat for our Saturday night baths, which we took in a large round galvanized metal wash tub.

My brother Stanley was a year younger than I, was quite active, and had trouble holding still, even long enough to get his picture taken. We played with simple things, because we didn't have many toys, so we made up our own games outdoors, playing hide and seek, etc. Mom always said I was like a clucking mother hen watching over my brother. He was my best friend growing up.

There, as a five-year-old, I went through a phase where I wanted to wear a head covering like my mom and Grandma Ollie wore, so Ollie humored me and made me one of Mennonite style without strings. I enjoyed Ollie's approval, which somehow, even at that young age, was important to me.

Mom made all my dresses that I wore for everyday and for church. The cheery yellow gingham one especially caught my five-year-old eye.

"Mama, can I wear the pretty yellow dress just once before Sunday?" I begged.

"No, Elaine; you'll get it dirty. That dress is just for church!"

My protests fell on deaf ears. I could hardly wait for Sunday to come, so when I had the chance and Mom was hanging wash out on the line in the yard, I decided to disobey her and put it on. I felt like a princess! Stanley just had to see my new dress. I was sure he'd like it too, so I hurried outside and headed for the side of the house.

"Ow, ow, help, help, help!" Shrieks and calls for help came from Stanley as I ventured outdoors. I forgot about my dress, and ran toward the cries for help, down over an embankment toward the farmer's pig pen. I slipped and fell on muddy grass, making a mess of my princess attire. Big sister that I was, I braved the displeasure of my mother, picked myself up, and went to Stanley's rescue. The crisis? He'd stuck his hand through the slats of a pig pen to poke a peaceful, dozing sow with a stick, and the enraged animal retaliated, grabbed Stanley's arm and swallowed it up to the elbow! He couldn't pull his hand out of the pen fast enough after he dropped the stick. He howled with pain as the sow bit down.

My feet lost no time in making a beeline for the house, muddy dress and all, crying, "Momma, come quick! A pig is biting Stanley's arm off!"

Mom grabbed the porch broom, took off on a run toward the pig pen, and when she reached it, let that sow know who was boss as she wielded her weapon across the pig's rump. The sow finally released Stanley, but the teeth marks were deep. I don't remember if my brother was taken to the doctor or not. Probably not, because Mom kept iodine, lots of bandages, adhesive tape, and salve on hand for Stanley's many mishaps. I, however, was dealt with because of my disobedience in wearing that forbidden dress. I think Mom made me "sit jack" on a stool for some time. Perhaps she didn't feel like being too hard on me, given Stanley's injuries and my copious tears.

On the sweet side of things, I was Mama's little helper. One day as she was washing dishes in the kitchen, I came to her and said, "Mama, I will walk into the kitchen and start drying dishes. Then you say, "My, what a good helper I have!" I left the kitchen, then walked back in, wearing a little apron she'd made for me. As I started drying the dishes, Mom humored me and followed through with her part in the play. I never forgot how I felt—so special and needed. My approval meter was pegged.

Mom surely had her hands full with us children, who numbered three at the Will Overholt tenant house.

My youngest brother, Sanford, was about two years old when he discovered a small metal can sitting in back on top of the unused old coal stove in the kitchen. He must have been thirsty, because he pulled down the oven door, climbed up to the top of the stove, grabbed the metal can, and took a swig of whatever was in there. Mom was in the next room at her sewing machine, and she heard Sanford choking and sputtering and gasping for air. She came running, and discovered he'd drunk some kerosene! We had no telephone, so she left Stanley and me, grabbed Sanford, and ran up the lane to the farmer's house to have them relay a message to have my dad come home quickly, and then she called the hospital.

The doctor said, "Whatever you do, keep him awake until you get here!"

Mom had someone stay with Stanley and me while Dad took Mom and Sanford to the hospital. Mom said he kept wanting to fall asleep on the drive there, but she made him stay awake. Once they arrived, the doctors pumped Sanford's stomach, and he eventually fully recovered. What a scare for my poor parents!

One day Mom was hoeing our garden and Stanley was riding his only tricycle; it had bent wheel rims and no tread on the tires. He rode off into Will Overholt's barn, then suddenly came pedaling back out as fast as he could. The farmer's big bull with horns was chasing him and was gaining ground rapidly. Mom fell to her knees, raised her hoe, and cried out to God to save Stanley; there was nothing she could do physically. Suddenly that bull just stopped dead in its tracks, turned, and went back into the barn.

I'm so thankful for a godly, praying mother and answered prayers!

The winds of change blew again, and my dad quit the Overholt tenant farming and took a job at Norfolk Naval Base as a bulldozer operator with the American Dredging Company. We moved about ten miles away to Court House Road to a two-story house with no plumbing, running water or inside toilets.

Our nearest neighbors at the end of our long lane were the Petrie's, so we called our house the "Petrie" house. Money was tight, but Mom always made the best of every situation. The linoleum floors were so worn there was no pattern left, and they anything but pretty. But Mom was resourceful, and she used left-over paint in gray, blue, yellow, and burgundy to paint the floor with a rag technique that made a pattern of sorts on the floor.

For heat in winter, there was a Warm Morning stove that burned wood and stood in the middle of the living room to heat the house, upstairs and down. Mom's washing machine again stood on the enclosed front porch, and there was a clothesline outdoors to hang up the wet laundry. I remember she also had a wooden drying rack. She had to heat water on our electric stove, then carry it in buckets to fill the washing machine. After the washing was done, she had to tote the wash water outside in buckets, walk to the back of the house and dispose of it.

Dad dug a well by hand, then put in a pump and water line so Mom could at least have cold water piped to the kitchen. That must have been an awful lot of work, but Daddy was always so good to Mom and was diligent to improve living conditions for us.

I have fond memories of the time Daddy built a large table, low to the ground, with little chairs to sit on so we could color and do activities for the three of us children. One day a big box arrived in the mail, and inside were many coloring books, crayons, and activities to do. We didn't have glue, so Mom saved the eggshells from breakfast and had us children dip our fingers in the leftover white of the egg to use as glue. It worked! Mom was the greatest!

Our large house had no basement, and Stan and I liked to play under the porch. I remember Mom checked our hair every night for ticks, which she frequently found. She'd heat the tips of a tweezers on our electric stove, and then carefully place the tweezers only around the tick, being careful not to touch our scalps, and the ticks withdrew quickly from our skin.

The Petrie property also sported an abandoned chicken house, and Stan and I made good use of it playing house. We set about making the place suitable for habitation by cleaning out piles of chicken straw and droppings, using a broom we found there. Clouds of dust and debris filled the air, and I soon was busy making mud pies and placing them on a board I placed at a forty-five-degree angle between two corner windows. As the sunlight baked my pies, Stan suddenly started wheezing and could hardly get his breath. I was really scared! I hollered for Mom to come quickly, and someone took him to the hospital where he was diagnosed with asthma. For years he had to sleep on a pillow filled with smelly hops. I felt so sorry for him. Thank God, he eventually outgrew the asthma.

Daddy talked often of a man named "Capt'n Bull" on his job, and I figured with a name like that the naval base must be an awfully tough place for him to work. Daddy told us about the time on the job he killed a huge snake as big around as his forearm! I was so impressed. I was equally impressed with the heavy bulldozer-shaped watch fob he wore on his belt.

There was no bathroom at the Petrie house. We had a Johnny Pot pail in a small closet in the hallway that we used when we had to go to the bathroom. When it was full, Mom or Dad carried it outside and dumped it into an outhouse. That way we didn't always have to go outside to do our "business." We had no bathtub. Mom and Dad filled a large, galvanized metal washtub with heated water and placed it in the kitchen for our Saturday night bath.

Stan and I shared a small cot in our parents' bedroom. How we managed, I don't know. My head was at one end of the narrow bed, and Stan's at the other; our feet shared the middle. Baby Sanford had a crib in their room, too. (How's that for marital privacy?) The only other bedroom was rented out to my Auntie Fannie's beau, Freddie Keffer, who worked in the area, and Auntie used to come visit us. (I wonder now where she slept when she visited us. Probably on the living room couch.) They eventually broke up.

One hot summer day, Stanley and I were playing in our cantaloupe patch at the Petrie house, when suddenly several wild pigs came charging toward us out of the woods near the house. Mom heard us scream, saw what was happening, and came running, brandishing the porch broom at those pigs. God surely must have anointed her weapon, because the pigs turned and ran away, and we came to no harm, thank God!

———————

I remember my first day of school at Kempsville Elementary; Mom dressed me in clothes she had sewn for me made from pretty, printed feed sacks. (Feed sacks were large cotton bags printed with designs and filled with grain for farmers' livestock). She also made a small feed sack lined white coat with little roses and a matching wind bonnet for chilly days, and I carried a gray and blue metal lunch box with a lid that closed with a latch. It also had a pint-sized thermos bottle.

Mom walked with me out to the end of our lane where the bus would stop, and I remember the tearful emotion I felt—probably coming from my mother too—as I waited for the bus that first day of school. I somehow sensed she tried hard not to cry, but instead she said to me, "Elaine, it's easy for you to make friends; I'll bet you will have a lot of new friends by the time you get off the bus this evening. You can tell me all about it then." And she was right! School was a strange new world for me, but I did make friends quickly, and it seemed everyone liked me. I'm sure Mom was praying for me.

Deuteronomy was not a word that should elicit laughter from a seven-year-old, but alas, I and a boy in the seat in front of me in class found it very funny one morning when the teacher announced she was going to read a passage from Deuteronomy. The word struck me as hilarious for some reason. We were disciplined for laughing, and she made an example of us in front of the whole room, saying Deuteronomy was in God's Holy Word and was not a joke. I think Teacher denied us the next recess period.

Speaking of recess, my favorite thing on the playground was the tall swings with double chains that extended from a center pole. There was an area for our hands to grasp a rubber strip between the chains as we ran along the ground, then swung higher and higher off the ground, body and feet dangling toward the earth. I loved that contraption and had lots of fun on it.

———————

Summers in Norfolk, Virginia, were so hot my dad could fry an egg on the hood of his car. We had a Kaiser-Frazer dark blue car with push buttons on the inside doors to open them, and I remember the seats were a deep bluish-purple plush velvet.

We went to church in that car every Sunday at Fentress Mennonite Church, where they had a Sunday School class for kids. We got little tickets with pictures on them if we could say our memory verses. One boy brought candy cigarettes to class one Sunday, and the teacher made him give one to each of us in class. I wondered if it was a sin to pretend to smoke a candy cigarette, and I was very timid about accepting one. Mom always faithfully read Bible stories to us at home and talked to us about Jesus, and good behavior was enforced.

I can still picture myself sitting on the church pew with my head leaning against Mama's arm during the sermon. I can still smell the scent of hominy frying in the kitchen of a house next door to the church. The odor drifting through the open church windows smelled so good and made my stomach growl.

———————

When we didn't have meat at home, Mom would make brown gravy to serve over mashed potatoes. She'd fry lard and flour together until it turned brown in a skillet, add salt and pepper, and enough milk to make a gravy. The thickened brown goodness tasted so good. We had plenty of eggs that we got from a friendly neighbor family who raised chickens.

One night during supper we heard a noise in the hallway outside the kitchen. My dad and Freddie Keffer investigated and discovered a large black snake had slithered up the rough wooden framework to a large wire basket that held our eggs and was about to help himself to our bounty! It was quite exciting to my young mind to watch my dad and Freddie as they captured that snake, disposed of it, and made me feel safe.

One day, Stan and I were in our large back yard playing near the large oak tree, when we heard a loud, angry buzzing noise. Upon investigation, we discovered a huge locust and monstrous wasp in mortal combat in the grass. I watched in fascinated horror as the huge locust succumbed to the wasp's sting and was dragged away, probably to a nest to feed her young.

I remember one Christmas at the Petrie house when my parents bought me a cute white plastic corner cupboard that had two shelves and hooks to display the little blue and white tin teacups, saucers, and plates. Stan got a large bouncing ball and seemed jealous of my gift. He pestered me when I tried to play with my tea set, so my parents put it up on a tall cupboard in the hallway outside the living room where neither of us could get it. All at once I heard a crash. Stan had thrown his ball at my tea set with very good aim and brought it crashing down. Part of the frame broke apart, and I was not a happy camper! But we usually always played well together and enjoyed doing crafts and coloring. Stan was my first childhood playmate, and I loved him. We always had a special bond. Maybe that's the way it is between the first and second sibling.

Chapter 3

Winds of change blew once more, and we moved back to Pennsylvania into a small tenant house in Summit Mills on Grandpa Claude's land. My dad worked for Grandpa Claude and eventually bought the livestock and machinery. Living conditions in that tiny house were no better than the conditions we'd left behind at the Petrie house in Virginia. We had to use the outhouse, and I don't remember much about that place, except that I was picked up in a car by Ervin Hershberger to attend third and fourth grades at St. Paul School near the town of Salisbury.

When I was ten years old, I went to fifth grade at Crossroads Parochial School started by Mennonite churches in the area. By this time, Grandpas had built a new house in a field above the farmhouse, and we had moved into Claude and Ollie's big farmhouse. A school bus picked up my two brothers and me and other Mennonite children in the area. I spent grades five, six and seven there, and had Miss Bontrager for a teacher.

I remember recess time and the highly competitive baseball games among the guys. We girls preferred to jump rope, and one girl, Naomi Peachy, was an expert at it. She was also a whiz at "high water, low water," where a rope was held taut by two people, and the height was gradually raised to see who could jump the highest, clearing the rope without bringing it down. Naomi was amazing! She could get a short running start, long skirts and all, and sail with ease over a rope held at the height of five feet! It seemed she had the legs and feet of a gazelle.

My teacher, Miss Mary Bontrager, read us the Little House on the Prairie series during story time after we came in from the noon recess. I especially enjoyed that.

The girls' bathroom was used at times for some young females to stuff their bras with toilet paper. I didn't wear a bra then, and I wondered why any girl would want to do that.

The girls made fun of my stockings that were rolled around a bulky elastic garter to keep them up at the knee. I was very self-conscious about it.

One of the older guys put small round mirrors in the slot atop his penny loafers, walked up to teenage girls (who of course wore dresses) and used the excuse of conversation to look underneath their skirts via the mirrors. I thought it most embarrassing and inappropriate, and made sure I stayed away from him.

At recess, we sixth and seventh graders conducted Carrom tournaments. What fun! I participated in many a tournament and was pretty good at the game. We used long sticks instead of the finger shooters that come with the game nowadays. (We have a Carrom game stashed in our garage today, but we never play it anymore.)

One recess when I and some others were in the school's furnace room in the basement, a dispute of some kind broke out between me and Lewis Yoder, an Old Order Amish boy. He dared me to stand my ground as he approached me, waving a tin can in his hand. I refused to back away, and Lewis cut me above the left eyebrow with the edge of the tin can. I was glad I didn't back down, and I think he was surprised that he'd struck me. I don't remember if the teacher gave me a band-aid or not.

As a seventh grader, icy winds of harsh judgment hit me from our school bus driver who chastised me for using the word "jeepers" as an expression of surprise on the bus ride to school. He pulled me aside when I exited the bus and sternly said, "Don't you ever use that word again!" Then he added, "And don't go telling the teacher about this, either!" I was crushed in spirit. I felt so awful, like I had done something terrible.

My approval meter was completely shattered.

Our teacher always led us in a hymn and prayer before we started school, and that morning of the school bus driver incident she chose the song, "Does Jesus Care" written by Frank E. Graeff. I began to cry even before we sang the words: "Does Jesus care when my heart is pained, too deeply for mirth or song, as the burdens press, and the cares distress, and the way grows weary and long? Oh yes, He cares, I know He cares, His heart is touched with my grief; when the days are weary, the long nights dreary, I know my Savior cares."

Years later, I found out that the Christian man (the bus driver) who chastised me had been found out having an affair with a married woman—this same man who demanded a strict compliance against using by words of any kind, even the words, "Oh boy!"

Eventually, the gentle wind of the Holy Spirit helped me to overcome my anger at his hypocrisy and I forgave him for the unjust pain he had caused me.

I remember how, at the close of each school day, we had to clean the blackboard, and once a week, we children took turns spreading a green sweeping compound onto the wooden plank floors and cleaned them with a push broom. I remember doing fractions and multiplication tables on the blackboard when the teacher called on me.

When I went to eighth grade, I attended St. Paul school, a small country school near the town of Salisbury, Pennsylvania. It was operated by Christian people, but oversight of the school was with Salisbury Elk Lick High School district. Elmer Maust was my teacher there, and I really liked him.

———

In ninth grade and through high school graduation, I went to Salisbury Elk Lick High. Having never been to high school, or seen anyone that attended there, I didn't know how to dress. Mom got me a new pair of women's shoes with chunky heels (I'll call them "Sunday shoes"), and some hand-me-down dresses, skirts, and blouses from bags of clothing my dad's sisters and mother received from somewhere.

I'll never forget the first morning I walked into my home room of that strange new school setting. Everyone was already seated, and many pairs of eyes stared up at me as I entered. I must have been a sight. I wore my hair parted on the side with a soft wave, my length of hair coiled into a bun near the nape of my neck. The bun was covered with a hair net and held in place with hair pins. I wore a white fine mesh Mennonite covering on top of my head, and a taupe and white polka-dot silky-like dress with a belt. My clunky shoes and nylon stockings held up by a garter belt completed the look. My feet were already feeling uncomfortable, and the school day had hardly begun.

There were four other Mennonite girls in the class, but only two of them wore a head covering like I did. There were a few Mennonite boys, too. I felt very much out of place, but everyone seemed to accept me as I found an empty seat. I remembered Mom's words to me years ago when I started first grade: "You make friends easily, Elaine." That helped.

Mom soon got me flat shoes to wear and made me some dresses.

PhysEd was an ordeal for me. Mennonites (at least, the ones wearing a head covering) didn't wear shorts—not even for gym class. So, Mom made me a pair of navy-colored shorts and a skirt to wear over them, along with a matching blouse. And then there was the disturbing issue of showering with a whole group of naked females. . . The PhysEd teacher eventually allowed me and the other Mennonite girls to use her private shower, for which I was so thankful.

That was the year my dad developed heart trouble and had to go to Shadyside Hospital in Pittsburgh, Pennsylvania for open-heart surgery. Mom went with him. I'll never forget the day we said "goodbye" to daddy. Through tears and a sinking heart, I watched him and Mama go slowly out the long sidewalk of the farmhouse into Grandpa Sam Beachy's waiting car. Grandma Lydia went along, as did Aunt Fannie, who stayed with Mom for the surgery. Sam and Lydia came back home the same day.

Claude and Ollie, dad's parents, took charge of us children. I remember one day I came home from school, saw Ollie and my aunts, Esther and Elsie, bustling around in the kitchen, up to their elbows in canning peaches or pears or applesauce—maybe all three. I was very tired, had an armload of books for homework, and I flung them down onto the counter of our large kitchen cupboard and dashed upstairs. I felt angry and frustrated and scared for Daddy who was in the hospital; I missed Mom. I threw myself on my bed and sobbed my heart out. I eventually had to come back down to go to the barn to help my brothers with the barn work and milk the cows, so I didn't have much time to dwell on how I felt. I know Ollie and my aunts knew why I behaved as I did, and I felt their sympathy. I remembered how I felt that special Sunday in our woods a few years earlier and how my heart had cried out to the Lord, *"Oh, if only those miracles in the Bible would still happen today! Why, oh why, had miracles passed away?"* Daddy surely could have used one.

Daddy finally came home. A hospital bed was set up for him in the living room and he slowly recovered. Mom resumed household duties, and also helped with the milking because Daddy couldn't work right then. After a few months, Daddy recovered and was able to do barn chores again; we were all so glad.

Then dear Mama suffered a nervous breakdown. She said the strain and stress of being alone for Dad's surgery in Pittsburgh exposed her to new and stressful conditions, even as she tried to be strong for Dad's sake. That, plus having her children on her mind, and the work that needed to be done at home, was just too much for her nerves to take. Mom told me later that every time she saw us come in from the barn in the morning, she felt like screaming and tearing her hair out. The doctor told her to get a lot of rest, and I think he gave her some nerve pills. Dad often took all of us up to "the clearing" on the farm where he had built a little cabin in the woods, and Mom would sit there just looking at the trees while we children played and sometimes had a hot dog roast.

Tenth grade was very hard for me because of Mama's nervous breakdown. I had to stay home from school and do the family laundry every Monday and help with other things too. I made "D's" in history and fell asleep in Mr. Slifko's science class more than once, much to my embarrassment. The other students laughed. At some point, Daddy hired a maid, Mary Garver, to help me with the work, and Mom gradually got better, but it took several years for her to return to feeling totally normal again.

I was called by my legal first name, "Miriam," in high school instead of "Elaine" as I was called by everyone else. Some students in my class called me "Smiley" because they said I smiled a lot. Maybe because I wanted to make friends—to feel accepted by my peers.

———————

For my sixteenth birthday, Mom and Dad surprised me with the gift of Aunt Fannie's 60-bass accordion that she brought home with her from Oregon. She used to play the instrument while she and Mom sang all kinds of songs with it. Auntie made me promise to keep it in the family, and I taught myself how to play it. In the evenings after supper, I'd take the accordion outside and play songs on the sidewalk so others could hear it too. Claude and Ollie, my paternal grandparents, lived just up the lane from the farmhouse we occupied—the house that had been theirs. I played and sang songs like *Mockin' bird Hill, Wildwood Flower, Church in the Wildwood, Distant Drums* (a Jim Reeves and Patsy Cline song), *Calm Nightfall, Smile Awhile, I Don't Know About Tomorrow, The Love of God, I Need the Prayers of Those I Love, What a Friend We Have in Jesus,* and *I'd Rather Have Jesus.* My family seemed to enjoy my music.

Dad also surprised me when he brought home a small ornate church organ with a mirror, foot pedals to pump the air across the pipes, and push/pull stops for different sounds. I taught myself to play hymns with shaped notes from the church hymnal. I wonder whatever happened to that organ. I felt loved by my dad because he bought it for me; I felt like he thought I had some talent for music. He himself had secretly played an autoharp as an Amish young man, but kept it hidden in the attic of the family home. Perhaps he wanted me to have the musical opportunity he was denied. I've often wondered how many God-given talents and gifts lay buried in the Amish church because people weren't allowed to play musical instruments, go further in education than eighth grade, or engage in business other than farming and maybe carpentry.

———————

I always had a weight problem, although not so much in my Junior and Senior years of high school. One afternoon as I came downstairs, I heard Dad and Mom talking in the kitchen. I paused on the steps to listen.

"Is she never going to lose weight?" My dad's despairing words of disapproval settled heavily on me. "You need to take her to a doctor and have her put on a diet."

I couldn't hear Mom's reply.

One day Mom told me she was taking me to the doctor to get a diet for me. I felt so ashamed. I don't remember the diet regime anymore, but I do know I was to drink milk with some vanilla in it. I hated milk, and don't like it to this day. Unless it has chocolate in it. I don't think the diet worked too well.

Dad also got me Metrecal powder mix for weight loss. I felt so humiliated and resentful, and I don't think I lasted long on that regime either. I felt like a failure.

As I turned sixteen and seventeen, I had a decent figure, but I still felt fat and was very self-conscious about it.

On Saturdays Mom and I worked in the kitchen together, and we always listened to the radio program *Unshackled* on WCKY, Cincinnati, Ohio. I distinctly remember one program I was listening to when the Holy Spirit spoke so clearly into my heart that I was no better in God's sight than that man on skid row. I had become a Christian already, but God gave me a humble, broken heart that day, and I saw the truth of what He said. There is no room for pride in the Christian life. Just because I was a "good" Mennonite and raised in a Christian environment did not mean I was any better in God's sight than that drunkard whose story I heard on the program. Everyone needs to be born again through Jesus and receive salvation.

My job on Saturdays, after the cleaning was done, was to scrub and cook a ten-pound bag of potatoes to use during the coming week. Mom made a lot of Amish fried potatoes and used the cooked potatoes in other recipes to feed our family of seven. By this time, I had four brothers: Stanley, Sanford, Marlin, and George, and everyone had hearty appetites because of the demanding farm work.

We also fixed desserts on Saturdays for the weekend in case we had company for Sunday dinner. One Saturday I was to make maple frosting for a cake, and I ignorantly used brown sugar with confectioner's sugar to give it flavor instead of using maple flavoring like I should have. I just didn't think. The icing didn't turn out well, but Mom didn't scold me. She just said, "Well, maybe we discovered a new recipe." I'll never forget how warmed and comforted I felt by her kindness.

I also remember the Saturday when I was about twelve or thirteen, Mom and I were at the kitchen sink together, and I happened to look out at the corner of a fenced-in area that bordered our lane. I saw one sheep trying to get on top of another sheep's back, and I was so surprised. I asked Mom, "Why are they doing that?" After a pause, Mom said, "He is trying to breed the female." That led to our discussion of the "birds and the bees." I found it a bit strange.

Mom surprised me one Sunday morning when I got dressed for church. I opened my closet door, and there hung a new rose-colored dress with little pink glass buttons on the bodice! I was completely astonished and overjoyed; I had never had such a pretty dress! I felt so special and loved by her.

———

Dad hired an Old Order Amish guy named Reuben Hershberger to help with the farm work. We soon found out he had a violent temper. One evening at milking time, he got so angry he threw a wooden broom handle so hard it went straight (and stuck) into the wooden door of the chicken house about fifty feet away. He slept in a bedroom in our farmhouse, and Dad put a lock on my bedroom door and told me to lock it every night, which I did. I felt protected and cared for by my dad. Reuben didn't last long as a hired hand.

———

Claude and Ollie had built a "dawdi" (grandfather) house several hundred yards above the big farmhouse where our family lived. I have splendid memories of trips up the lane to that house with my brothers to get some homemade bread and jelly. Grandma saw to it that we would never leave her house without her giving each of us a gospel tract. I knew she was a praying woman who cared deeply about the spiritual condition of her grandchildren.

I remember Christmases there with aunts and uncles and my cousins. I was always in charge of putting on a Christmas play with my cousins, and Grandma Ollie fastened a bedspread across the arched opening between the kitchen and dining room. We players wore bathrobes and head towels as we acted out the story of Jesus's birth. Some cousins recited poems or Scriptures they had used in their Christmas play at church as the adults beamed their approval.

Every summer, my aunts, Esther and Elsie, would host some "Fresh Air" kids from New York as part of their Beachy Amish church's outreach to city kids. I remember Sandy and Lorraine Berry, and especially Jenny and Carmen Rivera.

Jenny and Carmen were eventually adopted by Milton and Bertha Beachy. Jenny became a very good friend of mine, and because of her, I started dating David Beachy in my senior year of high school.

Chapter 4

I carried my lunch tray across the high school gym floor and glanced up into the bleachers. There sat a most handsome guy with black wavy hair and dark eyes. His eyes met mine, and I quickly looked away as I felt a slight blush creep into my cheeks. My heart seemed to skip a beat as I saw him look at me. The young man was David Beachy.

My friend, Jenny, soon deduced I had feelings for Dave when I asked her to invite both David and his twin brother, Jonathan, to our youth group activities. They all rode the same bus together and lived on the same farmland known as Beachy Brothers, but in different homes. Jenny's dad, Milton, was a brother to Dave's dad, Irvin.

She asked me, "Okay, Elaine, who is it? Which one do you like?"

I didn't answer, so she guessed, "It's Dave, isn't it?" When I remained silent, she chortled, "I knew it!"

I said, "Jenny, keep your mouth shut! Just invite them both to our youth group!"

She invited them all right, but she disobeyed me and told Dave that I liked him.

The night he and Jonathan came to the youth activities, Dave started paying attention to me. The next school day, he carried my books and walked beside me down the hallway to my eleventh-grade homeroom; I could feel the looks and hear the whispers of students as they noticed us.

What a strange, new feeling. But it somehow helped me to feel like I fit in for once. I felt approval.

Dave and I dated during my last two years of high school, but he dropped out halfway through his eleventh year because he hated the restrictions a lot of homework put on him; it cut deeply into time he treasured reading books. He chose instead to work on the farm and help his dad. He finished high school via correspondence courses and graduated from American School in Chicago. I was sad he quit school because I couldn't see him except on weekends. His twin brother, Jonathan, became a mail carrier for us. I wonder if Jonathan ever peeked into our missives.

———————

After I graduated high school in 1964, I applied for a bank teller job in Meyersdale, Pennsylvania, but didn't get it. Instead, I got a job at Flushing Shirt Factory in Meyersdale as a bander. Using high-powered commercial sewing machines, I sewed men's shirt collars to the bands that attach to the shirt, handling four pieces to fit together.

Dave got a job with Dutch Kolb picking up milk from Amish farmers for a guy who then hauled it to Queen City Dairy in Cumberland, Maryland. The finished milk products were brought back up to Meyersdale to be distributed there. When the regular driver to Cumberland sometimes couldn't do the route, Dave was designated to take his place, and he sure hated it. It was very stressful to find his way around in Cumberland streets. (Those were the days before such a thing as a GPS). It was also usually very hot when he had to make the run; he hated the heat too.

———————

After I was out of high school, my family sold their share of the Claude Yoder farm (cows and machinery) and bought a place between Meyersdale and Garret, called the Saylor farm, where he raised and sold grain. Dad also established a welding shop there called Yoder Welding. Dave had to drive a lot farther to come see me, but he said it was worth it.

In lieu of the military draft, Dave decided to enlist in the Mennonite program called Voluntary Service to serve his two years for 1-W credit. He wanted to get it behind him before we proceeded further toward plans of marriage. He sure didn't want to get drafted after we were married. I'll never forget the dark night as I watched him walk away from me and out to his car, knowing he was leaving to serve his two years of draft service. I had no idea when I would see him again. I cried.

On October 4, 1965, he left for Hannibal, Missouri for two years, during which time we wrote letters twice a week, and only rarely had a phone conversation because he couldn't afford it.

He got free room and board, but only made ten dollars a month the first year, and twenty dollars a month the second year. He worked in maintenance at Levering Hospital where he learned how to do a lot of things such as plumbing and electrical wiring. The money the hospital paid Dave went to the Mennonite Voluntary Service program. I was astounded he managed to save almost all his meager income, and only spent a little on things like toiletries.

He stayed in a house with others who were also in the Voluntary Service program, and they had house parents. Everyone shared in household chores.

Dave sang baritone in a men's singing group called The Kings Men Quartet. He preferred to sing bass, but another guy was already had that spot. They sang locally and traveled to some churches. I loved Dave's bass voice; it was perfection!

Oh, how I missed Dave. He came home for a visit in October after one year of separation, then six months later he came for another visit in April and asked me to marry him.

I still remember the night. As usual on our dates, we were sitting on the couch listening to records of singing groups at my house (probably the Norman Luboff Choir, which we liked) on the Saylor farm after my parents had gone to bed. I just knew he was going to ask me.

He began, "We have known each other for several years now, and I can't promise you riches or a lot of things, but I love you and want to spend the rest of my life with you. Will you marry me?

Of course, I said *yes!* I thought, "This is really happening! Wow!"

I also felt a responsibility settle on me; I can't explain it other than to say I took my *yes* very seriously. I wanted to be the best wife I could possibly be. Dave and I often prayed together on our dates, and I knew he was a wonderful, sincere Christian man I could trust. We talked about, and practiced chastity on our dates; that was very important to us. Why was it important to us? Because we knew God is against sex outside of marriage. We knew He wants us to be free of the trap of sin that brings sorrow and pain into our lives. You see, when a man and woman are joined sexually, they become one, as Jesus said in Mark 10:6 – 9 and experience a deep soul connection unlike any other. A connection that is meant to be experienced only in the sanctity of marriage and with only that one person. When someone is sexually promiscuous, or has sex outside of marriage, it damages the soul and cheapens the experience. God desires that we prosper in all things and be in health, even as our soul prospers. "Marriage is honorable among all, and the bed undefiled; but fornicators and adulterers God will judge" (Hebrews 13:4, NKJ). He will tell you that you are wrong, and wants you to repent, because He wants us to be whole and enjoy life. He knows what will hurt us.

For an engagement gift, Dave gave me a beautiful cedar hope chest he had made himself. (I still have all our love letters in that hope chest.) As Mennonites, we didn't believe in wearing rings—engagement or otherwise.

When he came home to stay that second October, he had nine hundred dollars saved since high school, and I had some money saved from working in the shirt factory. For the first year and a half, as was the Amish/Mennonite custom, I had given all my factory money to my parents, but my Grandpa Sam Beachy talked to Mom and Dad and said he thought they should allow me to keep my money when I got engaged. I was so happy he did that.

Chapter 5

My mom and dad somehow knew the owners of a half-acre plot of land just down the road from their Saylor farm and arranged for us to be allowed to put a mobile home on the property at no cost, because we'd be taking care of it. There was a well and electricity on the site. So, when Dave got home from Voluntary Service, we borrowed money from Citizens National Bank in Meyersdale, went to Somerset and bought a lovely brown/tan/cream mobile home called the Honeymoon Special. Oh, my, how I liked it! My very own castle!

I made my own wedding dress, and both dresses for my two twin bridesmaids, Ruth and Rhoda Metzler. We had a simple wedding at Springs Mennonite Church and had a simple reception in the church basement.

The morning of the wedding, November 10, 1967, Dave and I gathered pine boughs in Uncle Crist and Aunt Esther's yard in Springs and decorated the tables in the basement. My mom's good friend, Emma Maust, made our beautiful wedding cake and some fancy candles for the wedding table. I had baked some wedding cookies and we had very simple fare: small cartons of orange drink for kids, punch, potato chips, and sandwiches of some kind—likely chicken or tuna salad. I made fancy white chiffon aprons for all the waiters who worked in the church kitchen.

Stan, my brother and best man at the wedding, took pictures for us with his camera because we couldn't afford a photographer. I carried a white Bible with white streamers and small white flowers on top, and we had one bouquet of flowers at the church altar along with two tiers of candelabra and a unity candle. A unity candle has three parts: one central candle is lit by two smaller candles on either side by the bride and groom to symbolize two lives becoming one. That part was meaningful to us.

We couldn't afford a hotel room, so we decided to stay in our mobile home the first night. J&L, the company from which we bought our mobile home was to have electric and water hooked up for us before the wedding day, but somehow the water hookup was not made in time for the wedding. So, Stan brought a two-gallon thermos of water from Dad's house to our mobile home, and I think we had extra water for flushing the commode but am unsure of that. I don't know how we managed!

We got married on a Friday evening, and Mr. Fox, my employer at Flushing Shirt Company only gave me Friday through Monday off; I had to be back at work Tuesday morning. We didn't have money for a honeymoon, but Frank and Sue Keller, the house parents at the Voluntary Service unit where Dave had been in Hannibal, Missouri had a house in Lincoln Falls, Pennsylvania that they offered to let us use for a quick get-away. We took them up on the offer and set off in Dave's blue 1958 Chevy that his dad sold to him for one hundred dollars. Dave's dad, Irvin, had wanted to just give us the car, but Pennsylvania law said it was illegal to do that. Dave had to soon replace the transmission, which cost him seventy-five dollars. The windshield wiper motor and the radiator and heater core leaked too. He fixed those items himself.

I continued to work at the shirt factory which helped our financial situation. That place was a trial at times. The other girls in my banding section didn't like it that I could sew more piecework than they could, and they tried to make my life miserable. I had my thread cut more than once as they "happened" to walk by my machine and finagled to give me the largest sizes to sew to slow me down. They didn't want Mr. Fox to raise the quota we girls had to do to get paid a per piece bonus. They saw me as a threat.

Then there was the day I sewed my left forefinger. No finger guards were around the needle of those powerful sewing machines, and I happened to get my finger in the path of the needle, which went straight through my finger. I had to detach the needle from the machine, and one of the factory bundle boys took me to the hospital to get it taken out. He sighed and fidgeted when we had to wait, and I could tell he was none too happy with having been given the task of getting me medical attention. What was he griping for? He wasn't the one with a needle stuck through a finger. I think I went home after that, and the mechanics put a finger guard on all our machines from then on.

It was hot in the factory, too, because there was no air conditioning, and those high-powered sewing machines were operated by steam. In summer, I had to make multiple trips daily to the large sink near the restrooms and run cold water over my wrists for several precious minutes to keep from overheating. Minutes that took me away from my pursuit of making my quota and a bonus for the day.

The six girls were crude, and I felt their scorn when I wouldn't join in their trashy talk or unseemly behavior.

At Christmas time, one girl seemed to take special delight in the fact that she put an empty whiskey flask into my coat pocket, to made it seem like it was mine. I put on my coat to go home, felt something in the pocket, and pulled it out. Immediately the girls snickered and made some snarky remark intended to shame me.

The girls at the shirt factory seemingly felt no guilt about lying, being mean and ruthless. I prayed for them despite their false accusations against me. (Many years later I learned that the woman who'd sat next to me at her machine had become born again at the Grace Brethren Church in Meyersdale. I was overjoyed as she told me how grateful she was for her salvation. What a happy day that was for me as I realized my prayers were answered!)

That was the way the wind blew at work. More and more, I longed to just be a homemaker and take care of our little love nest at the Honeymoon Special. I wanted to start a family, and when I got pregnant in July of 1968, I worked for a few more months, and then only now and again when they were in a pinch. I never went back after Christmas that year.

Chapter 6

$\mathcal{I}$ loved our mobile home, and I loved being a wife and homemaker. We didn't have much money, but we never went hungry. I made a lot of my own clothes and helped Mom in her garden. Together we canned a lot of fruit and vegetables. Dave's first job was with my dad, Edwin, who paid him $1.25 an hour as a welder restoring dragline bucket teeth. After there wasn't enough work to keep Dave on, my dad learned that an Old Order Amish man, Alvin Summy (who Dave eventually learned was his first cousin because their mothers were sisters) was looking to hire someone to help with his carpenter business. My dad made connection for Dave, and Alvin hired Dave for $1.65 an hour, then soon raised it to $1.85 an hour. Dave picked up his boss on the way to work, because Alvin's church didn't allow him to own a car. But he could ride in one. Go figure. I thought the Old Order Amish rules were so inconsistent and without scriptural basis for authority. He worked for Alvin for a year and a half, then they both started working for Perry L. Yoder in Summit Mills. Dave had learned a lot about carpenter work, and Perry started him out at $2.00 an hour.

Our first-born, a son we named Douglas Edward, came into the world February 17, 1969, two months premature. That was quite an emotional experience for me. Because of breathing issues, Meyersdale hospital transported him to Memorial Hospital in Cumberland, Maryland. He appeared quite healthy when he was born, and cried lustily, but the doctor decided to put him on oxygen just to be safe. Doug developed Hyaline Membrane disease. I have read since then that too much oxygen given a newborn can possibly cause the disease to develop, but I don't know if that's true or not. I was not prepared for this. It felt like a bad dream from which I could not awaken. I was only prepared to bring my baby home from the hospital and had looked forward to caring for him.

The winds of desolation, fear, and sadness threatened me as I left the hospital without my long-awaited bundle of joy. The suitcase I had carefully packed with new and freshly washed baby clothes seemed to mock me in the back seat as we drove home. Questions and fears swirled around me as I got out of the car and walked with heavy heart back into our mobile home, carrying the suitcase. It seemed unreal that I was without my baby. Was Doug going to make it? Or would he succumb to the disease like the high averages indicated? I knew Dave's parents and my parents were also praying for Doug to make it, but the relentless cold wind of fear blew across my aching heart. My arms longed to hold him, my hands to touch him.

Dave and I drove to Cumberland several times a week to visit Doug in the hospital, where I could hold him on a pillow and feed him a little bottle, but I felt like I didn't get to touch him and bond with him like I could have under normal circumstances. He seemed so tiny and frail, weighing only four pounds, four and one-half ounces at birth. He was in the hospital for thirty days and was finally released to come home when his weight reached five pounds, eight ounces! What joy!

At that time, Dave and I didn't know anything about claiming God's promises for healing and standing in faith. I think now of my time in our woods that Sunday so long ago as a girl eleven years of age and the strange-sounding words that I spoke to God. And you know what? I believe those strange words could very likely have been powerful prayers of faith, prayed in a language I did not know, prayed years in advance of this much needed miracle in our lives! We do indeed sow seeds for our future with words we speak and prayers we pray for ourselves and our descendants!

The doctor put Doug on Similac formula, and he soon developed a nasty diaper rash that refused to clear up. He also cried each time after he had his bottle, as though he had a bad stomachache. We suspected the milk was the culprit. I boiled his diapers after I'd washed them, and applied creams from the doctor, all to no avail.

I called our doctor. "Dr. Berkebile, Doug still has this awful diaper rash; we've done all you told us to do, but he's no better. I hate to see him in pain. Could we please try to change his formula?"

Dr. Berkebile replied, "No; Doug's body just needs time to get used to the formula, and he'll soon be okay."

But he wasn't, and I was very upset.

Finally, one morning after weeks of Doug was so miserable, Dave took matters into his own hands, went to Thomas Drug Store in Meyersdale, and bought SMA formula. He had read that SMA has a different protein, nearer like mother's milk than Similac. Doug's problems cleared up immediately! We rejoiced as winds of gladness breezed through our little home.

Because Doug was two months premature, I stayed out of church with him for a couple of months to allow him to grow stronger and his immune system to develop properly. One Sunday morning when Dave was at Rock Church in Meyersdale, I was feeding a bottle to a very sleepy baby Doug. It was time for his liquid vitamin drops, so I carefully squeezed a little bit on the inside of his cheek so he wouldn't choke on them. I don't know what happened, but suddenly Doug started to choke and couldn't get his breath.

I panicked. What should I do?

I cried out, "Jesus, help me!" I instinctively put my hands under Doug's arm pits and raised him heavenward, giving him to Jesus.

Suddenly Doug gave a loud gasp and swallowed, then started crying. Best sound ever! Oh, how I thanked God for helping me—a new, inexperienced mother all alone with a preemie. Doug was able to finish his bottle and was fine. Thank you, Jesus!

Our daughter Debra was born in October of 1970 and our happy little family of four lived in our Honeymoon Special for a little over four years.

Chapter 7

A fresh wind of the Holy Spirit was about to blow into our lives. When we got married, we attended First Mennonite Church in Meyersdale, PA, although we used Springs Mennonite Church for our wedding ceremony, and Ross Metzler, our pastor at First Mennonite, had married us at Springs.

Several months after we were married, a man we knew, Lloyd Yoder, invited us to attend a Full Gospel Businessmen's meeting in a neighboring town. We didn't know much about the group, but we had heard they believed in speaking in tongues. We consented to go with them to the event, even though my parents were not too pleased and spoke against it. They believed the organization was in grave error about all this Holy Spirit stuff.

At the meeting, numerous people stood and gave testimony about how the baptism of the Holy Spirit had impacted their lives. As I sat there with Dave, I became highly offended. *I'm as good a Christian as they are; I don't need to have this thing called the baptism of the Spirit!* I was nervous and upset, and yet everyone seemed like sane, reasonable people. I don't know what I expected these "full gospel" people to be like. I had heard terms like "holy rollers," which conjured up a shameful image of a people possessed with something not quite so holy.

On the way out the door from the meeting, there was a table set up that offered free books. For some reason, the book, *Aglow with the Spirit* by Dr. Robert Frost caught my eye. *This guy is educated; he has a Dr. by his name. He won't say anything kooky about this Holy Spirit stuff.*

I hesitated, then quietly picked up the book, took it home and put it in my dresser drawer.

Curiosity about the book filled my thoughts. As Dave was at work one day, I decided to pull out the book. I settled myself on the little brown couch in the living room of our mobile home and began to read.

As I read, I received understanding and the Holy Spirit stirred my heart. And on about page seventy-something, I got on my knees beside the couch and asked Jesus to baptize me in the Holy Spirit! I was weeping as the wind of the Holy Spirit blew away my pride and softened my heart. I began to pray in tongues by faith, just as the book had said I could do. Oh, I felt so good and free! Fellowship with the Holy Spirit was so real and wonderful. I had entered a new dimension in my Christian walk with Jesus! The book had said this experience opens the heart to believe and understand God's supernatural ways of the Holy Spirit.

Then I heard Dave's car in the driveway. I quickly got up and put the book back into my dresser drawer and wiped away my tears. I didn't tell him what happened to me but started dinner.

I can still see myself standing at our little kitchen sink washing the supper dishes that night when fearful thoughts came. *Elaine, you have really sinned! You spoke in tongues, and you know it's of the devil! Even your dad said so!*

My insecurity and panic buttons were both pushed.

I didn't know what to do. I certainly couldn't confide in Dave. In desperation, I left the kitchen, went back into our bedroom, shut, and locked the door. Then I got down on my knees beside the bed, crying out to God to help me overcome this attack of fear. I did the only thing that came to mind: I prayed in tongues as fervently as I could! And you know what? Fear left me. Peace came, and I knew my experience had been real. I had no one I could call for help, but the faithful Holy Spirit held my heart and caused me to realize this was an attack of the devil against me. The wind of the baptism of the Holy Spirit was real and powerful! It defeated the devil's attack!

As I gathered my courage and shared my experience with Dave, he too began reading the book, and was also baptized in the Holy Spirit with the evidence of speaking in tongues.

———————

Eventually, I shared my experience with my mom, and she too read the book and received the baptism of the Holy Spirit. My dad, bless his heart, had an exceedingly difficult time with her experience. It had been ingrained into his belief system that this was of the devil.

One morning I got a phone call, and it was my dad. He was crying and desperately distraught. He choked out the words, "Elaine, Mom is kneeling on the kitchen floor, and she's talking really strangely. I don't know what to do! Can you come help us?"

We lived just down the road from my parents, so I hurried up there right away. I found my dear mother kneeling beside a chair, praying fervently in tongues.

Dad asked, "What is wrong with her?"

I replied, "She is praying in tongues, and is distressed about something."

I interrupted Mom's praying to ask her, "Mom, what is wrong?"

Between sobs, she revealed that Dad had rebuked and challenged her when she tried to tell him how wonderful the baptism of the Holy Spirit was.

Mom said, "Daddy said he feels like he isn't even married to me anymore. I was so hurt, and all I could think of to do was to pray."

I was shocked to my core by what Daddy had said, and I could tell Mom was deeply wounded. I explained to Dad what was happening and assured him she was okay. Dear Dad was crying, and my heart went out to him as well. After a bit I was able to share with him my experience and the truth of the reality of the Holy Spirit baptism and encouraged him to read the book for himself and see what he thought. He did read the book and eventually also had the blessed experience. I was overjoyed that the wind of the Holy Spirit had blown into his heart as well.

Chapter 8

hen winds of adversity blew against us. The owners of the plot of land where our Honeymoon Special mobile home was set up were members of the Brethren Church in Meyersdale, and we learned that somehow word got around to them that we had embraced the baptism of the Holy Spirit with the evidence of speaking in tongues. They came to our mobile home one day and were none too friendly when they told us we had to leave the property, saying, "We have use for the land." We knew by the Holy Spirit why they wanted us off their land: they didn't want people like us on their property.

I was distressed to leave the comfort of having my mother close by and distressed at having to find another place to call home. We decided to sell our mobile home and look for a house to rent, and eventually moved to Lura Folk's house in Springs, Pennsylvania. I remember how I stood that one lonely, last day in our empty Honeymoon Special and said goodbye to our little haven. The tears flowed freely, and in my heart was a deep pain—not only the pain of losing our beloved Honeymoon Special, but also the pain of rejection by our Christian landlords.

And the lot where our mobile home had been stood empty for many, many years.

We were attending First Mennonite Church in Meyersdale when all this transpired, and I shared my book, *Aglow with the Spirit,* with Mildred Faidley who also received the baptism of the Holy Spirit. I was elated!

(I lost track of my original book; who knows where it is today? I loaned it to someone who never gave it back, and I don't know any more who it was. I have often wished for it back, but was able to buy an expensive original copy with yellowed pages from Amazon a few years ago.)

There was a lot of contention and unforgiveness among some of the dwindling membership at First Mennonite, and Ross Metzler, our pastor, said as long as there is unforgiveness in a church, it won't grow. He left, and the church closed its doors.

———————

Meanwhile, some Beachy Amish young folks from Mountain View Amish Mennonite Church had also experienced the baptism of the Holy Spirit (imagine that! – but then, God is no respecter of persons) and started meeting together at the home of Dave's parents, Irvin and Tillie Beachy. We were soon invited to attend these "Hungry Hearts" meetings, and the living room was always packed with people hungry to experience God's power and presence. Words of knowledge flowed, along with prayers for healing, testimonies of answered prayers and what God was doing in people's lives. I will always be grateful to Irvin and Tillie for also having a hunger for the things of God and opening their home to us young people.

God was faithful to provide good fellowship for Dave and me. And since the First Mennonite church building was now vacant, the "Hungry Hearts" group under Emanuel Miller's pastoral leadership (his wife, Miriam, was my first cousin) bought the building, as I recall, and formed Rock Church, which we attended when Doug and Deb were quite young. After some time, they installed Ron Plaskov from Virginia Beach, Virginia, as pastor, but after a while it was discovered that he was abusive to his family. What a shock that was to us! He was eventually terminated.

A man from Pittsburgh whom I will call Nelson Johnson, came to visit at Rock Church, but it turned out he led several families into error with what was called the shepherding movement and influenced them to sell their homes and property and move to Pittsburgh to join the church he had there. He demanded full allegiance to his leadership. They were not to question anything; they were told if those in leadership (the shepherds) were wrong, God would correct them. Thank God, He kept us, and both sets of our parents from deception, but we felt quite torn apart from those we loved and with whom we had been in such wonderful fellowship at Rock Church.

The winds of church turmoil seemed to be everywhere we looked. Then for a time, we and both sets of our parents fellowshipped at Holsopple Church of the Brethren, where Raymond Mankamyer was pastor.

There, I remember the intense emotional pain I suffered that was caused by misunderstanding what was meant by a "love feast" for communion.

My mother-in-law, Tillie, told me that the church didn't just have the token bread and grape juice, but they had a sit-down meal with roasted lamb, bread, gravy, and other things. In my mind, it was equal to a fellowship dinner, and was to be held of an evening at the church.

I asked Tillie if I should bring anything, and she said, "No, the ladies of the church prepare all the food."

I thought, "How lovely!" So, we as a family didn't eat supper that evening, although my children were hungry. I told them we would eat the fellowship meal at church.

When we got there, we sat patiently waiting a long time to be called around the tables to eat.

My heart sank when I saw sparsely laden tables with just enough food for a few bites per person. My heart pained for our children who were so hungry. To make matters worse, I soon learned that most of the women frowned at me for allowing our children to come to the table at all to eat a bit of the Lord's supper. I felt awful. Like my chest and insides were going to burst from grief. I could barely eat anything. I felt judged and so very out of place. Rejected. I could hardly wait until the foot washing was completed and we could get out of there. My friend, Mary Alice Mankameyer, wife of the pastor's son Clay, tried to console me, saying God wouldn't mind if my children ate because they were hungry. But the women of the church surely disapproved, and I still felt bad.

I cried most of the way home, and then I fed our children properly when we got there. I felt like I had failed my children—subjected them to an awkward position. And I felt like an outcast, whispered about because they dared eat from the Lord's table.

Chapter 9

I don't know how much that situation at the Holsopple Church of the Brethren influenced our decision, but after a while, Dave and I decided to leave there and join Springs Mennonite Church where we had been married, even though we felt very much out of place there too. We knew they didn't welcome the baptism of the Holy Spirit. Nonetheless, we thought maybe God could use us there to be a voice for Him and a good influence to help introduce the wonderful experience of the baptism of the Holy Spirit to others.

Before we were allowed to join, the elders asked us to meet with them.

As we walked into the church basement that evening, it seemed like we were facing a tribunal court. All the elders sat in a semi-circle in front of us.

"We're here to talk to you about becoming members of our church," one elder began.

Another elder said, "We hear you want to join the church in order to change it."

We looked at each other as it became obvious through further conversation that they were suspicious of our experience with the Holy Spirit.

Change their church? Well, not exactly. We certainly would not be pushy or obnoxious, but neither would we be silent if the subject of the baptism of the Holy Spirit ever came up. We wanted to be where God put us, but after all, we were still Mennonites. Holy-Spirit baptized Mennonites. Ah, there was the rub. A source of friction to some. They saw us as an irritant, but we were glad they allowed us to join the church. We didn't know where else to go.

I was asked to be a song leader there some Sunday mornings. I remember how we sang acapella, and I used my pitch pipe to start on the right note. I raised my right arm to begin the song and motion of the beat: four-four time, three-four time, or two-two time.

There were a few in the church who were somewhat interested in the baptism of the Holy Spirit, and we shared our experience with them.

Strangely, the biggest resistance to sharing our beliefs came in the Sunday School class we attended when we told them it was God's will that all be healed as well as saved. Man, that drew some heavy fire! I remember sitting there more than once, feeling nervous, shaky, and so unwelcome. But the wind of the Holy Spirit blew through us anyhow as we shared the truth of God's Word on healing and the baptism of the Spirit. One person remarked to me after one class, "I feel like I've been taught today." Praise God! That cheered my heart.

One Sunday after church a lady practically forced a book on me, saying, "This will prove that it's not always God's will to heal!" It was a book based on someone's experience with sickness. *Why do people elevate their experience with sickness as though it was gospel above what God says about healing?* I didn't want the book, so before we went home, I went down to the church basement to put the book back into the church library, only to find the lady who had given me the book talking to someone else. From across the basement area, she looked up when she saw me, and quit talking. My people-pleasing button quivered under her gaze.

We were active in church life at Springs Mennonite, sowed a lot of spiritual seed there, but it was not up to us to produce a harvest. I always felt like an outsider. Maybe that's what we were. Not of one mind and heart with most of them. I got a lot of practice keeping my love on there. And I had to lean into God for approval—not people.

At our home in St. Paul, Pennsylvania, I loved to share with family and others what was called the word of faith teaching we had learned through well-known ministries like Andrew Wommack, Joyce Meyer, Charles Capps, and Kenneth Copeland, among others. We had learned about speaking God's word in faith, believing and standing in faith for healing, and the Holy Spirit baptism. Dave and I enjoyed glad, sweet fellowship together with some of my family members as we shared our testimonies with them and met at their home regularly for Bible study. and they were very open to receive what we shared.

But one day my mind reeled with deep shocked disbelief and grief when I learned they didn't want to be with us anymore. A man from out of state told them they must break off fellowship with us and hear only him.

Those dear family members walked out of my life—maybe forever? *Surely not, God. Please, Father, let it not be so. Bring them back into fellowship with us. Please watch over them.*

My mind tried to take in what had just happened. It seemed like a bad dream; surely this could not be happening! Cold, cruel winds of pain blew through my heart and soul, and I felt so crushed and desolate. Rejected. Dumfounded.

Although very deeply hurt and concerned about the deception they'd stumbled into, we could pray, even as we tried to think of ways to reach out to them. Their home remained closed to us (and everyone else, too) for many years. However, we continued to love them and pray for them despite the painful rejection we'd experienced. We realized that Satan was the one who comes to steal, kill, and destroy, and the real enemy was not my dear aunt and her family, but the evil spirits behind those actions.

But more about this later in chapter twelve.

Chapter 10

When we lived in St. Paul, Pennsylvania, between Meyersdale and Salisbury, we learned of a Charismatic church called Indian Lake Center near Stoystown, and left Springs Mennonite Church. Even though we had to drive forty-five minutes one way to attend there, it was worth it! Finally, we had Christian brothers and sisters who believed in being filled with the Holy Spirit and speaking in tongues, in healing, and all the gifts of the Spirit. What a gift to have unity!

Dave and I had been introduced to Amway by Allen and Mary Otto while we were still members at Springs Mennonite, and they became our sponsors in Amway! We were surprised that at the rallies they encouraged us to buy books by Kenneth Copeland and other "word of faith" teachers. And even though we never made it big in Amway, God used it to change our negative "stinkin' thinkin'" as they called it, to thinking and speaking words God could use for good. We came to understand the power our own words had in shaping our lives.

One day I went on the road to try to get some sales and stopped at a stranger's home to introduce her to the Amway products I had in my case. As I stepped into their house, I learned they were Eli and Catharine Sommers, a couple (and their two girls) who attended Maple Glen Mennonite church.

I spotted a book by Kenneth Copeland on their dining room table.

"Do you know Kenneth Copeland?" I asked Catherine in surprise.

Catharine's mouth and eyes flew wide open, and she exclaimed with excitement, "Do we know Kenneth Copeland? Do we know Kenneth Copeland? I should say we do! We have most of his books and tapes! We have gone to his meetings; he is such a blessing to us!"

I was dumbfounded. My mouth dropped open. Here was a Conservative Mennonite woman (wearing a large Mennonite head covering) and her husband, telling me that they loved Kenneth Copeland—a tongues-talking, faith-preacher of the Gospel!

Well! That started a fast friendship as our hearts were knit together on the spot. They too felt out of place in their church. Soon, we started meeting every week in our home for Bible study. What a blessing and source of strength that was to us! Dave and I learned true Bible faith by reading Copeland's books and listening to his Scripture-filled teaching tapes.

Our relatives were resistant to the truth that it was always God's will to heal people. I shared how Jesus came to show us the Father, and Jesus only did what He saw His Father do. Jesus went about doing good and healing all who were oppressed of the devil, for God was with Him, Scripture says.

But years of religious teaching are not easily washed away. We soon found ourselves in conflict with our families who held firmly to the "if it be God's will" teaching, citing Paul's thorn in the flesh as proof that God does not always want to heal people. They had been taught, as we had been, that God said *no* when the apostle Paul asked God to remove the thorn (which they presumed to be an illness). It was such an assault on our faith as Satan tried to steal God's word out of our hearts. The winds of opposition brought tears and heartache, and yes, division.

Let me just state here that now I am established in the truth. I saw that when one reads the entire chapter of 2 Corinthians 11 in context before getting to chapter 12 and verses 7 – 9 about Paul's thorn, one can easily see that Paul's thorn was severe persecution. He endured shipwreck, beatings, physical dangers, etc., that were sent by a messenger of Satan to make things rough for him wherever he went. Satan did not want Paul to be received with honor (to be exalted) nor his message believed. Also, using the law of first mention in Biblical interpretation, the term "thorn in the flesh" appears in the Old Testament at least three times, and each time it refers to people as thorns. Numbers 33:55, for example, states, "But if you do not drive out the inhabitants of the land from before you, then it shall be that those whom you let remain shall be irritants in your eyes and thorns in your sides, and they shall harass you in the land where you dwell." Judges 2:3 and Deuteronomy 7:16 are other examples.

God does not control people; they have free will, and Satan inspired people to come against Paul. But God said His grace was enough to empower Paul to use his spiritual authority to overcome all these hurdles. The Lord taught Paul that "The weapons of our warfare are not carnal, but mighty in God for pulling down strongholds" (2 Corinthians 10:4). Paul had the authority to bind and loose, and the authority and privilege to co-labor with God in the earth. When he was stoned and left for dead, the disciples gathered around him, prayed over him, and he got up and walked into the city. Angry, religious people were always thorns in his side. God also showed him that "We do not wrestle against flesh and blood, but against principalities, against powers, against the rulers of the darkness of this age, against spiritual hosts of wickedness in the heavenly places" (Ephesians 6:12).

But at that time years ago, the painful battle between faith and doubt regarding healing waged war in my mind. Who was right?

One day as I was ironing in my dining room, all these oppositions and heartaches swirled within me, and I cried out to God, "Is the faith message real? Please show me the truth! If it's Your will to always heal, please show me that. If it's not, show me that too. I want the truth!"

As I wiped the tears from my cheeks, I decided to go to the living room to turn on the radio for some music, to put something pleasant into my mind. As I turned the dial, a man's voice suddenly caught my attention. He was teaching on God's will to heal! *Who is this guy? Where is he from? What station am I listening to?* I continued to listen and was amazed. It seemed every question I had about healing was being answered. Forgetting my ironing, I put my ear up close to the radio because there was some static, and I wanted to be sure to get this guy's name. As he went off the air, I was disheartened by the fact that the only thing I caught were the call letters of the station. I quickly wrote them down and wondered how I could contact this speaker.

Then I got the thought to phone the Directory Assistance Bureau at 1-800- 555-1212; I told the operator I needed the phone number for that radio station, and she gave it to me. When I dialed the number, I told the man who answered why I was calling and wondered who that person was on his radio show just then. He checked and told me it was Andrew Wommack!

The station guy asked, "Where are you calling from?"

I replied, "I'm in a little town called St. Paul in Pennsylvania."

He inhaled sharply with astonishment, then declared, "There is no way you could have received our radio signal from where you are. We are only a small radio station in Texas!"

I knew then and there that God had indeed supernaturally answered my heart's cry. The wind of the Spirit had carried that radio signal all the way from Texas to our humble house in Pennsylvania to answer the cry of my heart! He had given me the desire to turn on the radio for some music so I wouldn't feel so sad. The miracle was cemented in my heart forever.

Long story short, I contacted Andrew Wommack Ministries from the information I was given and received many of his cassette tapes for free when we didn't have the money. My hungry heart was fed, and I was so grateful to become more established and rooted in the truth.

God brought new friends into our lives too: Forrest and Linda Miller from Meyersdale who had befriended Dave's parents at a Russ Bixler healing meeting. We invited Forrest and Linda to join Eli and Catharine at our house for weekly Bible studies to strengthen one another—a practice we continued for several years. God brought us into fellowship with others who were hungry to experience God's supernatural power in their lives as well. We were hungry for God's power to be displayed through signs, wonders, and miracles. The world still needs them!

I remember one day after we had met for Bible study in our home the night before, our neighbor, Lilly Brown, approached me in the yard and said she saw flickering candles in our living room window the previous night and asked me what that was. I was so surprised I didn't know what to say other than "I don't know." There had been no candles in our windows. I tucked her comment into my heart and wondered if perhaps the Spirit of God graced us by showing up as a candle flame in our window. Our little group prayed some powerful prayers of faith together.

Chapter 11

*A*t our St. Paul house, I had a sewing business doing alterations, making men's suits, bridesmaid's dresses and more. Dave lost his job with Puff's Mobile Homes because the business shut down, so he had to find work somehow to provide for our family. I remember we couldn't make our house payment of $180 per month, and I called the bank and told them our financial situation. I also sent a letter explaining that we will pay just as soon as we are able, and I found out later that the Citizen's National Bank had clipped that letter to our file and given us grace. I thanked God for their kindness.

I remember standing in our kitchen with Dave and declaring God's promises for our financial provision as we struggled with giving the tithe from whatever money came in. We were also told by someone that it isn't God's will to prosper us financially. We should have just enough to get by. How discouraging. *If we only have enough for ourselves, how can we ever help anyone else? How can we give to ministries in need?* We kept on standing on God's promises that showed it was His will for us to prosper.

Then one day Dave found out that John Coleman in Berlin, Pennsylvania, wanted to build a log house, and Dave was able to get the job along with our oldest son, Doug, who was now out of high school. That led to other jobs, and Dave was self-employed for about five years, doing whatever jobs came along. We kept standing on God's will that we would "prosper and be in health even as our soul prospers."

One of those jobs was to wallpaper a house in West Salisbury. The day before Thanksgiving, Dave took me along to help him when the kids went to school. We worked hard all day and I came home so tired and still had to get dinner on the table for our family of five. As I was preparing dinner, the phone rang, and a lady asked if I had her pumpkin pies ready to pick up. Oh dear, no! I had totally forgotten I'd promised a week or two earlier to make four pumpkin pies for her! I was trying to help make money wherever possible. I was so stressed out. I worked until late into the night getting her pies baked. And as I recall, I was to make some food for my own family's Thanksgiving get-together with my parents, brothers, and their families the following day. I guess it's just one of those times when you put one foot in front of the other and keep going. The Holy Spirit empowers one to keep on keeping when we must.

My garden always did well, and despite all the hard work, I loved seeing the shelves in the basement fill up with canned peaches, pears, applesauce, green beans, tomato juice, pickled beets and cucumber pickles. I also had a strawberry patch and froze sugared mashed strawberries. It saved money on the grocery bill.

I had leisure time too. I remember how, after the children were on the school bus to Mountain View Christian School, I'd get all my work done by the time the soap operas came on TV at one o'clock in the afternoon. I sat and watched those things for several hours until the children came back home.

One day as I was watching them, the thought came, "It wouldn't be so bad to have an affair." The alarming thought shocked me wide awake. It was as though God pulled back a curtain and let me see what would happen if I ever made such a choice: my beautiful marriage would be destroyed; my children would be decimated; I would bring shame on Dave's family and my entire Yoder family, not to mention upon myself! I was horrified! I turned that TV off, and I have not watched a single soap opera since that day!

The faithful wind of correction by the Holy Spirit blew into my conscience. And I learned this: be very careful what you give your attention to, what you read, see, and hear. For that which you allow into your life will impact and shape you for good or evil. The seeds you plant in your mind and heart will produce a crop unless they are uprooted. You can cut off bad thoughts or feelings from yourself by declaring, "I take authority over that thought/feeling in Jesus's name and renounce it. I place the blood of Jesus over it, cancel it and command it to be destroyed." God warns us in Proverbs 4:23, "Keep your heart with all diligence, for out of it spring the issues of life." The devil will slip a thought into your mind whenever he thinks he can. It is imperative that we give him no room for invasion!

I became involved with the Women's Aglow Fellowship chapter in Somerset, Pennsylvania, took part in the board meetings and held offices within the organization as well as later becoming president of the Somerset chapter for one year. I was the speaker for one meeting and played my accordion and sang. It felt so good to be among sisters in the Lord who taught and encouraged the baptism of the Holy Spirit and all the gifts of the Spirit. My good friend Catherine Sommers also attended, and sometimes rode with me. Several of us girls always had lunch together afterward. I remember my aunt Elsie attended one meeting as well.

A bright spot for our children was when my sister-in-law, Barb, brought a little Chihuahua puppy to the house one evening. She had been to a yard sale, and this little female was the runt of the litter with a protruding belly button of sorts, and nobody wanted her. Barb felt sorry for her, and took her, hoping that our family would give refuge to the outcast. She was so little, her front and back feet fit on the palm of my hand! I wondered if she was even weaned, so we offered her some milk in a saucer, and she lapped it right up. We decided to keep her, at least until Dave got home from work to see if he would give his approval. I don't think he was too keen on having a dog in the house but seeing how the children were so enamored with her, he consented. We named her GiGi. She brought the children much delight, and our son Doug especially bonded with her. I had to put down pee pads for her until she learned to go potty outside, and everyone had to help in her training.

When she got bigger, there were times she wandered off into our neighbor's field and rolled in cow manure. She came marching home, looking quite proud of herself, like she thought she smelled wonderful.

I got the worst of the manure off outside, then took her upstairs into the bathtub to finish the job. After she was clean, she'd race around through the house like crazy in fast twists and turns, up and down the stairs, and back again. When I saw the joy she brought the children, I couldn't stay mad at her for long. She was a big part of our lives and gave us many a laugh.

GiGi also liked to go into the garden with me and pluck green beans off the vine and chew them as green juice ran out of her mouth. She loved to chase rocks when the children threw them, and she always found them too, carrying them triumphantly in her mouth as she came trotting back to the thrower. Sometimes the rocks were so big, she almost tipped over from trying to carry them. I was amazed she got her small mouth around them! She was with us for eighteen years, until I had to have her put down. That was awfully sad.

I remember one Sunday morning when we were getting ready for church, fourteen-year-old Doug came downstairs wearing casual clothes—a pair of jeans and a T-shirt. I was upset with him and told him he had to go change his clothes for church, but he opposed me. We had a battle of wills as he insisted it shouldn't matter what he wore to church.

The Holy Spirit helped me to see his point of view, and by this time we were both in tears. We sat on the couch together there in our living room in the St. Paul house and I told him I was sorry for arguing with him and asked his forgiveness. He also apologized to me, and we gave a tearful hug to one another. I realized later he was trying out his "growing up" independence, and I was so glad I gave in to him rather than insist he did what I wanted. I also realized later that the main reason I had been upset with him was because I didn't want anyone to think of me as a bad mother for the way my children dressed. There was nothing wrong with what he wanted to wear; it was clean and neat. I was in the wrong. I am glad for the wind of the Holy Spirit to correct me!

Eli and Catherine Sommers introduced us to the ministry of a man named Percy Collett, who had been a missionary to the Amazon jungle, and who made a series of cassette tapes about his supernatural trip to Heaven. We were so blessed to be able to go with them to hear him speak at a church, and we bought the album of tapes. I played those more than once and was so blessed by his witness. He spoke of things that are also mentioned in Scripture. I loved his descriptions of what he saw and experienced while there for five and a half earth days as the Indians watched over his body as it lay on the Amazon jungle floor.

Percy told of the beautiful streets of gold and the mansions that are there, of the wonderful music in heaven. There were huge pianos and trumpets and all kinds of instruments, and he could play them! He spoke of animals in a part of heaven. He saw where aborted babies are kept and cared for in the heavenly nursery, and how they grow. He saw a procession of little children carrying a small bunch of flowers to signify that they had forgiven their earthly mothers for aborting them, and so much more. (If you'd like to hear him for yourself, most of his tapes have been put on YouTube which you can search out for yourself.)

How excited I was to share Dr. Collett's testimony with people! (I like to share things I enjoy—be it natural or spiritual food.) However, not everyone I talked to about Dr. Collett's testimony wanted to hear it. I sensed they thought such reports from heaven couldn't be real. But that's okay. The healing wind of the faithful Holy Spirit comforted and refreshed me.

Chapter 12

Work became scarce for Dave, who had been self-employed for five years, but we kept on standing on God's will to prosper us. My uncle, Sam Beachy Jr. had moved to Virginia, and started his own backhoe business there. His son, Jeff, was also in Virginia and got work with Scott Long, a commercial construction company. One Friday when Jeff got his paycheck from Scott Long, there was a note in the envelope from Bruce Scott, one of the owners, asking if Jeff knew of any other people from Pennsylvania who were looking for work.

Jeff immediately phoned Dave to ask if he was interested! Dave and I talked about it and decided this was God's way of prospering us, and thought we perhaps should move to Virginia where the work was. So, Dave said *yes* and called Bruce Scott yet that Friday night and set up an interview for the following Monday. He was immediately hired as a carpenter with only a phone interview! We knew it was God's blessing for our finances!

The next day, Tuesday, Dave prepared to leave for Virginia. Wow. Talk about a sudden shift in my equilibrium! I was a mixed bag of emotions. I was so glad Dave would finally have good employment, glad for how God had honored our standing in faith for prosperity, but oh how I felt the responsibility of my new role. I realized I would be at home alone with the children all week to tend to all their needs. Dave would come home Friday nights and leave again Sunday afternoons.

Dave arranged to stay with my brother George and his wife Barb who had also moved to Virginia already, as had my parents and my other three brothers and their families. I was the only one of my family left in Pennsylvania with my little brood. How I looked forward to Friday evenings! We all rejoiced to see him come down the road in his blue Matador.

Saturdays were spent doing Dave's laundry and fixing food for him to take to Virginia. I regularly made French toast and sometimes Egg McMuffins for his breakfasts and sent along lunch meat, bread, and other goodies for his lunch box.

In winter, it was up to me to fire the coal furnace and, with the help of our children, carry out the ashes to the back of our property onto an ash pile. I did it, and kept the family warm and fed.

Then after a few months, Doug decided he wanted to go to Virginia and work with Dave, so Scott Long hired him, too, and put him on the same job as his cousin Jeff; both were laborers.

Now it was just Deb and Darren and me at home. I remember how Deb and I stripped the large upright piano and refinished it. We had many good times together, but I also remember how we wiped tears as we watched Dave and Doug drive away every Sunday afternoon, and they probably had a few tears as well.

We had been attending Indian Lake Christian Center where Dan Nicholson was pastor, but Dave and I decided to have "church" at home on Sundays because of his short stay with us, with him having to go back to Virginia around three o'clock. I know there were people (they told us so) who thought we should still make the forty-five-minute drive to Indian Lake and forty-five minutes back, which would have barely given us time to eat Sunday lunch before Dave and Doug had to leave.

A good friend at Indian Lake didn't think the Lord wanted us to move to Virginia, and said, "You don't want to go, only to find out later that it was a huge mistake." Now there was some confusion in my mind about it, so I prayed for God's direction. One day as I was outside at our house, I looked up into the sky, and saw a huge cloud in the shape of a person wearing a garment, and it looked like a hand was coming out of a sleeve, pointing south. I stared and wondered about it before deciding that it must be the hand of the Lord pointing us South!

By this time, our daughter, Debra, had fallen in love with a young man named Keith Yoder, the neighbor's farm boy. I'm sure she had some painful mixed feelings about moving. She missed us being together as a family, but she also wanted to date Keith.

After a while, we contacted a realtor in Virginia to look for a place for our family to live and sold our St. Paul home ourselves. Talk about a move of faith! We moved to Virginia before we went to closing on our house in St. Paul. But God worked it all out! We found a half-acre on Yorkshire Lane and put a new modular home on it. I felt like a queen! It was beautiful, and Dave provided so well for us. The front lawn and landscape were lovely, and our whole family enjoyed the back porch, large gazebo and hot tub deck Dave built off our dining room door in back, as well as Doug's hot tub. Doug and Darren helped him build all those structures, and a large wood shop for Dave in one corner of our lot near the gigantic oak tree. For several years I had a small garden just beyond the oak tree.

The first year we lived at 8908 Yorkshire Lane, we attended People's Church pastored by Larry Andes, founder of Fishnet Ministries. We chose to attend there because they were a Charismatic church such as we had been accustomed to at Indian Lake in Pennsylvania. My parents and all my brothers and their wives attended Manassas Assembly of God. People's Church had no youth group because it was a newly founded church. We met in Stonewall Middle school on Lomond Drive and had to set up chairs for every service and take them down again. I'm not sure how it came about, but our son Darren started going to the youth group activities at Manassas Assembly, and really enjoyed it because he had an outgoing personality and needed interaction with others his age. And since we valued Darren's needs for youth fellowship, we decided to leave People's Church and become members of Manassas Assembly of God.

It was nice to see my family at church Sunday mornings, but before long it became evident to Dave and me that our belief in the "word of faith" teachings weren't exactly welcomed there either. We believed that speaking and standing on God's Word in every life situation was vital and powerful in receiving God's promises for ourselves—to stand on what God said and enforce Satan's defeat won by Jesus at Calvary. To give Jesus the reward for His suffering.

I remember someone speaking derogatorily of our beliefs as being of "that name and claim it club." I felt rejection and wanted to leave Manassas Assembly. But we stayed, really because we didn't know of any other place we could go.

We didn't have much money beyond what it took to pay our bills, and I remember feeling wistful Sunday mornings after church as I watched my parents and brothers with their families go out to lunch together. How I longed to also go out to lunch with them. In time, as God prospered us more financially, we and our children were able to accompany them. And we did have family get-togethers from time to time, which helped our need for social interaction with others.

I watched Joyce Meyer a lot on TV and bought many of her teaching tapes and videos as well as her books. She was a big part, along with Andrew Wommack, in helping my faith to be strengthened. I played her teaching tapes throughout the day as I worked in the kitchen. I will always be thankful for her, and for her candor in sharing her testimony of how she came from being sexually abused by her father to be a teacher of the Word who is known world-wide. I will always also be thankful for how God led me to Andrew Wommack Ministries; I also played his tapes a lot.

I often felt lonely. Everything in Virginia was so strange and new. The road traffic was heavy, and I had to learn to cope with it. We had moved from a very rural place in Pennsylvania where some of our neighbors were Amish, and the pace of life was much slower. I had been involved in our church at Indian Lake, at Women's Aglow ministries, and had weekly Bible studies with Eli and Catharine Sommers as well as Forrest and Linda Miller. I had been president of our chapter of Women's Aglow in Somerset. Here I was a "nobody." I didn't fit, I didn't belong.

Dave, Doug, and Deb all had jobs, and I was a stay-at-home mom who home-schooled our youngest son Darren from ninth grade through his senior year.

One evening shortly before Christmas, as we sat down to eat dinner, Dave, Doug, and Deb joyously announced the. Christmas bonuses they'd each received from their bosses.

Self-pity raised its ugly head in me. *Where was my bonus? Didn't I work too?* I pinched back the tears and left the table in pretense of getting something in the kitchen. I asked the Lord to help me be truly glad for their good news. I realized that Dave's bonus also benefitted me; but besides that, I also realized while I may not receive monetary value for my work, God valued me. And the interaction between me and my children had much value as well. There are some things money can't buy.

Sometimes I had to squash self-pity like a bug after I'd spent several hours preparing an evening meal for the family, only to have them eat in fifteen minutes what had taken me hours to prepare. Often, Doug, Deb and Darren went to their rooms and sometimes Dave went to the living room to watch TV, leaving me alone with a table to clear and a sink full of dirty dishes. It's at those times that the wind of the Holy Spirit came to play softly across the strings of my heart to produce a godly attitude. The Holy Spirit doesn't condemn: He corrects in love; He lifts and heals.

One evening I discovered a large lump in my left breast. Fear washed over me even as I tried to comfort myself. I talked to Dave about it and wondered what I should do: should I go see a doctor? Was it just a hormone thing (as I was starting through menopause) or was it the dreaded "C" word? Dave said I had to do what I felt God was telling me to do. Everywhere I went it seemed I heard talk of cancer. A fighting spirit rose in me, and I decided I was going to pray! Every morning I knelt at our blue armchair in the living room and prayed in tongues against that lump. I commanded it to be gone, in Jesus' name. I rebuked it. I stood on my healing from Jesus, quoting Scripture: "By Jesus' stripes, we have been healed" (I Peter 2:24). During the day, I would often thank God for my healing from Jesus. I did this for what seemed to be many weeks—I'm not sure anymore how long it was.

One morning as I got up from prayer, I heard these angry words in the air in front of me (though not audibly): "Come on! Let's go!" and I distinctly sensed the intense hatred of three evil spirits as they passed in front of my face and headed out our front door as I held it open, commanding them to be gone, in Jesus's name. I was not scared, but I knew those evil spirits had been at work. I don't remember anymore how long it went until the lump disappeared, but it went away. A few months later I had a mammogram, and all was clear! Glory to God! Praying in tongues is part of the wind of the Holy Spirit and is healing and powerful!

———————

We kept on praying for my dear aunt and her family who had disowned us so many years before. Eventually we heard they'd moved to Georgia.

One day as I was on the treadmill in the basement of our Yorkshire home in Virginia, the phone rang on the wall next to the treadmill.

"Hello?"

I was delighted to hear the voice of my dear aunt! "Hello, Elaine. I wanted to call while we were still alive and able to do so and ask your forgiveness for the way we treated you in Pennsylvania. It was wrong of us."

"Oh my dear one! It is so good to hear your voice! And we forgave you a long time ago! You are certainly forgiven. I have missed you all so much! What a blessing to have our friendship restored! How is everyone?" We had a blessed conversation.

The whole Yoder family decided to have a reunion after my aunt's family opened their hearts to us again. It is my recollection that the evening before the reunion was to be held, Claude was told that the whole family was coming. The stunning thing is that the morning of the reunion, as everyone was arriving for the reunion, Grandpa Claude just quietly went home to be with Jesus. I really believe when he heard the good news that the entire family was gathering together, he knew his prayers had been answered. He went to heaven that morning, one week before he would have been ninety-six.

The family stayed and we all ate and fellowshipped together.

Years of praying, and praying in tongues, never giving up, had a powerful effect. Two of my cousins in my dear aunt's family eventually went to Andrew Wommack's Charis Bible College! All those years of separation are dissolved, and we are, once again, one in heart and mind. What a blessing!

Chapter 13

Our daughter Deb married Keith Yoder on November 18, 1989. I had the privilege of making her wedding dress and her bridesmaids' dresses. We were very close, and now the house seemed so empty without her in it anymore. But we had many good times together with family get-togethers, hot dog roasts, holiday celebrations and hot tub parties (thanks to Doug's hot tub) on the rear deck.

Then Darren and Melanie got married September 28, 1996, and he moved out of his bedroom. Doug took advantage of the opportunity to have Dave help him add Darren's room to his to give him a nice big bedroom. He needed every inch of space because he also had a treadmill, large TV, large desk, and computer equipment in his bedroom.

There was a small fridge in the basement in the family room, but Doug really needed more space. The laundry area, canning shelves, water heater and furnace were all in the basement. So, we decided to begin looking for another place to move to where he could have the whole basement to himself. If the three of us bought a house together, it would help Doug by not having his own mortgage payment, and it would help us to make a much larger house payment.

Deb and Keith were blessed with a beautiful baby girl, Alissa Rose, on August 3, 1997, and I was needed to baby sit her when Deb had to go back to work three months later. Deb brought her to our Yorkshire house, and we added a crib in the bedroom that had been Deb's. I baby-sat her for three and a half years until Deb gave birth to their second daughter, Nicole Anne. I have such fond memories of babysitting Alissa; I formed a strong bond with her.

As time went by, we readied our house to put on the market and decided to save realtor's fees and list the house ourselves. I must say, we had an attractive, well-kept place, and there was a lot of buyer interest.

My family knew we were house hunting. One morning my sister-in-law, Barb, called and said a realtor had just posted a "For Sale" sign on the empty lot that joined their back yard! I immediately got into the car, drove to Weems Road, wrote down the number on the sign, and called it. Turns out they were Christian people and already had house plans drawn up to have his aging parents move into the upper level while they themselves would live downstairs. Long story short, we ended up buying the lot for $187,000 and they gave us their house plans! The year was 2002 and the house plan was perfect for our needs! God is so good!

Then in the summer of 2002 when Dave was having his blood work done to apply for insurance coverage, they found that his PSA count was up. I had no idea what PSA was, and I asked the insurance lady what that meant. All she would say was that Dave needs to go see a doctor.

I became suspicious that something serious was up. They found prostate cancer. That was quite a challenging time for us. I can still see us sitting there together at our dining room table in our Yorkshire home as each day Dave and I spent time in the Word and took communion together. We stood on God's Word for his healing.

His doctor referred him to a specialist for treatment to get radioactive seeds implanted directly into the prostate to kill the cancer. God brought us through that time of crisis as well. He had the procedure, and God helped us through the whole ordeal.

This old world is such a battleground! Satan comes seeking whom he may devour, and he comes only to steal, to kill, and destroy! But thank God, Jesus came to give us life, and life more abundantly until it overflows, as scripture says in John 10:10.

That summer, we had also found Golden Rule Builders in Catlett who would build our home for us. They were in transition within the company, and the result was lack of diligent leadership to get our house built.

Every day Dave would come home from work, and after dinner we drove to our lot so he could oversee the job himself, often doing two days' work in one (all the while dealing with prostate cancer and treatment). Time dragged on; heavy and prolonged rains brought the building process to a standstill more than once, and we were frustrated.

Meanwhile, we were showing buyers through our Yorkshire house, trying to sell it. We soon sold our house at an excellent price, for which we thanked God. We didn't close on that house until our new one was ready to move into. I loved our Yorkshire house; it was the home Dave had worked hard to provide for us. I had such rich memories there, including the years I spent being involved in Home Interiors & Gifts and doing shows in our home and other people's homes in the area as far away as Bealeton, Virginia.

My dad's heart was giving him trouble again; he'd had his third open heart surgery about ten years earlier. When Dave and I worked on our new house on Weems Road, I would go across the back yard to visit Mom and Dad. Those were special times for me, and Dad was able to see the foundation go up at our new place. But much to my sorrow, he passed away in early April of 2003. He never got to see us move into our new house that joined their yard.

Chapter 14

After we moved to our beautiful new home on Weems Road in February of 2004, I entered a very painful and desolate three years of my life when my nervous system suffered a bout of clinical anxiety/depression. What a strange and unreal world it was. I supposed that all the stress and strain of the previous two years took its toll on me, but I also blame the strong medication I was given for bronchitis.

A nurse practitioner had put me on 500 mg of Cipro three (or maybe four) times a day, a strong antibiotic that caused me to break out in huge itchy welts all over my body. Shortly after that, I began with clinical anxiety. I couldn't enjoy our new home, nor could I enjoy the people I loved. It was a very hard time in my life indeed. But the Holy Spirit never left me. The Lord told me to go on medication from my doctor, which I did, and eventually I overcame the condition.

My sister-in-law, Shirley Yoder, was a comfort and help to me. And it was she who suggested I start a women's Bible study in my home after I was better, which I did. It helped me, too. I had a wonderful group of women from Manassas Assembly of God (later called Chapel Springs) where we attended, some of whom received the word of faith belief I shared, and the group lasted for several years.

At Chapel Springs Dave and I were given the opportunity to start a small group when the church held a campaign to begin new groups. We became leaders of a class we called "The Upper Room," which we led for about five years and had many wonderful times of fellowship together.

We began to feel the tug to find another church home and struggled for two years over whether we should leave the church; but we also loved our small group members and the fellowship we enjoyed with them.

I remember one Saturday around Christmas, 2013, I was getting a load of laundry together. As I lifted the basket onto my hip, I suddenly had a breakthrough of surrender to the call of God to leave Chapel Springs. I leaned my free arm against the door frame of the closet, lowered my head onto my arm, and just wept. I said *yes* to God, and my surrender was accompanied by a liberating sense of freedom.

It was scary to think of leaving the familiar, to not have a church home anymore. I shared my experience with Dave, and he agreed it was time to leave. We made an appointment with the pastor of Chapel Springs and went to see him, explaining that we felt the Lord was leading us to a different church fellowship. The pastor was gracious and wanted us to come to church one last Sunday (which would have been after the New Year in 2014) so the leadership could present us to the congregation and thank us for our years of service and involvement there, and to pray over us. We didn't feel we wanted to do that, but rather wanted to make a clean break at the end of 2013 and start the new year afresh in a new place.

Our daughter's family was still at Chapel Springs, and so were two of my brothers and their families. It was hard to leave them too, but the winds of change from the Holy Spirit compelled us to leave.

A year earlier, because of a friend, I had knowledge of a church called Living Faith in Manassas. Her daughter had taken some classes there and loved it so much. On a whim, I had decided to search them out online and saw they were offering classes on codependency, and it sounded like something I needed. I signed up online, having never met the people or gone to the church. I finished the ten-week course and really enjoyed it;

and best of all, I discovered they strongly believed in the word of faith teaching like Dave and I did!

We had no plans to attend there, and indeed, did not know where God wanted us. We had heard of another church in Fairfax that sounded like what we were searching for, so the first Sunday in 2014 we drove there. We were there less than an hour when we both just sensed this was not the place, even though they were also a "faith" church. We whispered to one another about leaving right after worship and try to make it to Living Faith Church in Manassas by 10:15, so we left as discretely as possible.

I felt a hesitant anticipation as we drove into the church entrance to an unimpressive gray storefront building with the large blue letters, Living Faith Church.

When we walked through the doors and heard the worship, we looked at each other through misty eyes and said, "We're home."

Epilogue

We learned that Pastor Barry Lubbe had come from South Africa many years ago in obedience to the call of the Lord to start Living Faith Church. He had run Kenneth Copeland's ministry in South Africa, and had quite a large, successful, and flourishing church there. He left it all behind, and came across the continent with his wife, Joan, and three teenage children to a strange land and began a small house church in Amissville, Virginia with just a handful of believers. The church grew and eventually they bought the store front buildings where the church is now at 10266 Battleview Parkway, Virginia.

Pastor Barry passed away about two years ago, and his son, Gavin, took over the ministry.

As of this writing in 2021, we have been at Living Faith Church for over seven years. The Lord has continued to use us as we led several different groups for a time in a marriage seminar titled "Love and Respect" by Dr. Emerson Eggerichs on Wednesday evenings. Later we started a group called "Connections" that meets Sunday mornings and is ongoing.

I attend a women's Bible study group on Tuesdays called "Women's Life" and Dave attends a men's group once a month on Saturday mornings.

Living Faith Church is our answer to a search for fellowship with those who believe in miracles, signs, and wonders—the full Gospel of Jesus Christ. Besides sound, biblical teaching, there is dynamic, meaningful worship, and words of knowledge and prophecy are frequently given. Prayer team members stand ready to pray for healing or any other needs after each service. The gifts of the Holy Spirit are in operation, and I have been so encouraged and blessed by the Lord there.

I wrote and published six books in the past ten years. The first three are a trilogy for children using a rabbit family as characters; I have had some mothers tell me how much they helped in relating to their own children, and some wished they would have the books earlier when their children were growing up. The titles in the trilogy are *Biff and Becka's Springtime Escapades, Biff and Becka's Stupendous Vacation,* and *Biff and Becka's Splendiferous Christmas.* The next book I wrote was a devotional titled *Journal Gems: Nuggets from My Heart to Yours,* and the book that soon followed that one is titled *Rhyme and Reason, A Collection of Poems and Short Stories.* I also published a cookbook, *Elaine's Kitchen: Made from Amish Stock.* All my books are available on Amazon. (By the way, if you buy my cookbook, there is one error for you to note. It's the recipe for Egg Custard, page 72, and should include the ingredient 1/3 cup sugar. It would have cost me over seven hundred dollars to correct it.)

I still have my 60-bass accordion today, and once in a great while I'll get it out of the worn red velvet lined case and play something on it. Dave made a recording of my singing and playing songs I mentioned earlier in this book and put it onto a CD.

Life is not free of challenges, and we are still standing firm in our faith for some things; but I am so thankful for the stability God gives us through His promises. The word of faith teaching, blown into our lives by the wind of the Spirit, has proved invaluable!

Let me add something. Just because we are born again and have been baptized in the Holy Spirit, does not mean we live a life of perfection. Growth and revelation are a process, and we need to give grace to one another. There were times when I was wrong.

It was Friday, October 23, 2015. As usual, I got out of bed and went about minding my own business. As I sat in the bathroom, I was thinking about various things—WestBow Press, my book shipment, my plans for the day, etc. Suddenly, around my stomach area, I heard these four words that seemed to come from within: *two days without meals.* The voice was very deep and loud, authoritative. That was it—then silence. Nothing else followed. I was stunned.

What was that? Was it God? Was it the devil?

After a minute or so of consideration, I felt condemned because my weight has always been an issue in my life. I felt guilty.

I don't want to go two days without any meals. What about eating something when I need to take aspirin for pain? But I'm not going to ask why. No one should ask God why when given a command. But is it God? Maybe this is how the Father's voice sounds, and maybe Jesus and the Holy Spirit's voices sound like the still, gentle promptings and thoughts I've been used to. But maybe it was the devil. Which was it? I was confused.

I didn't ask my trusted Christian friends at Living Faith Church or even my wonderful husband for input. I didn't ask my doctor if that would be okay for me. I decided on my own that it had to be God. *After all, I need to lose weight, and God must be displeased with me.* A few days later, I decided to go two days without meals. I told myself that maybe God was elevating my spiritual experience with Him. I tried to feel spiritual about it, but I was glad when those two days were done.

As the next week approached, I was so afraid I'd hear that voice again, hear the same command again. I lived in dread of it. So, I decided to just go ahead and fast two more days every week until I felt free to stop. And that's what I did. For almost a year. It wasn't easy. And I hadn't lost any weight worth mentioning—maybe five pounds.

Then December 18, 2016, I came down with diverticulitis with a small rupture, which landed me in the hospital for three days, right before Christmas. I'd never, ever had diverticulitis before and didn't know why I had such terrible pain. Looking back now, I can see how such sporadic eating created adverse conditions in my intestinal tract. I was given strong medications in the hospital, and upon discharge, was told by a nurse practitioner to take MiraLax daily for four months for my intestinal health and was to be on a diet free of seeds and such things as corn to make sure I didn't have a recurrence of diverticulitis.

About four months into taking the MiraLax daily, I developed clinical anxiety/depression, a chemical imbalance in the brain. I wouldn't wish it on my worst enemy. I did some research after I realized what was happening, and I discovered that indeed seventy percent of women over the age of sixty also developed clinical anxiety/depression from the MiraLax! I learned that MiraLax was polyethylene glycol, an ingredient used in brake and transmission fluid in vehicles! I also learned MiraLax had been banned in Europe a few years earlier. I was incredulous. I told my doctor and stopped taking it (it's now on the list of things I'm allergic to). Instead of MiraLax, I simply started using Metamucil and bran cereal. A few months later I had to go on medication for clinical anxiety/ depression. It's been a little over four years, and by God's help I am doing ever so much better but am still on the road to full recovery.

To combat the anxiety and lies that wanted to fill my mind, the Holy Spirit gave me scriptures to stand on in faith, and I wrote the verses and encouraging words of truth from Him on 3 x 5 cards and taped them to the backsplash of my kitchen where I could see and say them often. I fought the good fight of faith, and others were praying for me.

I thank God for our Tuesday women's Bible study group at our church. In 2019, we were going through a book titled "The Prophetic Voice of God: Learning to Recognize the Language of the Holy Spirit" by Lana Vawser. God used that study to help me in a powerful way to realize that the deep, authoritative voice I heard that morning of October 23 in 2015 was definitely *not* God! I had followed the wrong voice, and the fruit of it led me down a path of hurting my own body, causing diverticulitis. Then I was told to take MiraLax that caused the clinical anxiety! What a sad chain of events!

Lana Vawser showed how the fruit of the devil's voice is confusion and condemnation, lack of clarity, lack of peace, and fear. Wow, that surely described my situation! To the contrary, the fruit of hearing God's voice is peace; it's empowering and strengthening. He never contradicts His Word, and His voice always reveals His nature. I learned that when we're growing in our understanding of the voice of God and how He speaks, we must pay particular attention to the *fruit* of what we are hearing. The enemy will always leave you questioning. The voice of the Lord will always leave you with peace, not confusion. It's all about the *fruit!* Thank God for the Holy Spirit's revelation of the truth! Peace and freedom came.

Now I am wiser because I have received the counsel of other godly women and authors like Lana Vawser. We dare not be an island unto ourselves, or we are headed for trouble. We need other sincere, mature believers, for they have been given insights into godliness by their own experiences and the Word of God.

The Holy Spirit has also recently led us into more revelation about heaven and God's ways, especially using a godly woman, Kat Kerr, among others, who we found through Facebook. God commissioned her to be a Seer from the time she was very young and has taken her to heaven thousands of times during her life. Her testimony is that she is completely sold out to God, saying only what He gives her to say. What a blessing to hear what heaven is like, and what God says to her for our benefit here on earth! She is now seventy years old. She is the middle child of fifteen children and has written two books titled "Revealing Heaven I," and "Revealing Heaven II". Her third book is about to be published. She is also on YouTube.

It is because of what she taught Dave and me about heaven that I can truly rejoice and not feel sad that my dear mother, at the age of ninety-six and a half, passed from this life into her heavenly home on February 26, 2021. I know she and Daddy are having a spectacular time!

I marvel when I look back and see how the wind of the Spirit blew upon my life down through the years, leading me from the Mennonite tradition to greater truth and freedom into what is called the Charismatic experience. I am so blessed that my husband Dave shares the experience with me!

To God be all the glory forever and ever!

How To Be Born Again

Ever since Adam and Eve sinned in the Garden of Eden, mankind has needed to be restored to God's fellowship. God never stopped loving us, but our sins separated us from God. No matter how good we may try to be, our own efforts are rubbish compared to God's holiness, God's standard of perfection to put us in right relationship with Him. Indeed, "There is none righteous, no not one" (Romans 3:10). And "All have sinned and fall short of the glory of God" (Romans 3:23).

But there is good news! "For God so loved the world that He gave His only begotten Son, that whoever believes in Him should not perish, but have everlasting life. For God did not send His Son into the world to condemn the world, but that the world through Him might be saved. He who believes in Him is not condemned, but he who does not believe is condemned already, because he has not believed in the name of the only begotten Son of God" (John 3:16 – 18).

All you need to be born again (made righteous) is to have a humble heart to acknowledge that you need Jesus to forgive you of your sins so you can have His gift of righteousness credited to you. God tells us, "If you confess with your mouth the Lord Jesus and believe in your heart that God has raised Him from the dead, you will be saved. For with the heart one believes unto righteousness, and with the mouth confession is made unto salvation. For the Scripture says, 'Whoever believes on Him will not be put to shame" (Romans 10:9 -11).

Pray this simple prayer: "Jesus, forgive me of all my sins. I believe that You paid the price for my sins to be forgiven, and I believe God raised You from the dead. I declare that You are my Savior and Lord. Thank You for saving me. Amen."

Be sure to tell someone that you have received Jesus as your savior and find a good church to attend—a church that believes in the baptism of the Holy Spirit and the gifts and miracles of the Holy Spirit. I would be glad to know if you invited Jesus to be your savior; you can e-mail me at elainesplace4@verizon.net. Welcome to God's family!

The Baptism of the Holy Spirit

Questions Christians sometimes ask about the baptism of the Holy Spirit:

- What is the baptism of the Holy Spirit? <u>See Acts 1:8.</u>
- Didn't I receive the Holy Spirit when I became born again? <u>Yes.</u>
- Do I have to pray in tongues? <u>You get to.</u>
- Why should I receive the baptism of the Holy Spirit? <u>We are commanded to do so. See Ephesians 5:18 – 20, John 7:38, and I Corinthians 14:1.</u>
- Are tongues always the evidence of being filled with the Holy spirit? <u>See Acts 2:4 and Acts 8:14 – 17.</u>
- What are the benefits of praying in tongues? <u>See Jude, verse 20 and Romans 8:26.</u>
- Isn't there danger of receiving an evil spirit when I pray in tongues? <u>Luke 11:9 – 13.</u>
- Isn't this something scary or weird? <u>Not if you know what God says about it.</u>
- Is it necessary to my Christian experience, and if so, why? <u>Yes, because you pray the perfect will of God when you pray in tongues and also gives God perfect praise.</u>
- Aren't tongues a gift that is not intended for every Christian? <u>Acts 2:1 – 4, they all spoke in tongues. In a public church service, some have the gift of tongues which are accompanied by the gift</u>

of interpretation so all may be edified. Every Christian should experience tongues for private worship and prayer.

- What will my family and friends think of me? <u>Matthew 10:37</u>

The power of the Holy Spirit is for you today! The same Power that moved upon the dark, empty, void, and shapeless mass of chaos called earth (Genesis 1:1 – 3) and brought forth order and beauty and life is available for power in your life. You can live life to the full (John 10:10) and enjoy God's Kingdom as a son or daughter of the King!

1. Truly be aware of your need; repent of any sin the Holy Spirit brings to your mind, and humbly desire the fullness of the Holy Spirit in an attitude of prayer. Ask Jesus in child-like faith for the baptism of His Holy Spirit.

2. Begin to thank God for the gift of the infilling of the Holy Spirit and ask Jesus to baptize you with the Holy Spirit. Be assured, according to Luke 11:13 that you will not receive a counterfeit experience. Submit and release any pride.

3. Focus on the Lord's presence with thanksgiving in your heart and ask Him to give you a prayer language. Worship the Lord, tell Him how wonderful He is.

4. Begin, by faith, to speak any sounds (even "baby-like" utterances) that the Holy Spirit brings to your thoughts, and don't worry if you think they may be manufactured by your mind. The Holy Spirit works through your mind, and you speak with your mouth, moving forward by faith and humility. He will not make you speak. Don't try to figure it out intellectually. He will anoint you to speak more and more fluently as you continue to pray in tongues. You build yourself up in your faith as you do (Jude 20).

5. Pray in tongues daily as you come to your prayer and fellowship time with God. Don't stop with a one-time experience, and think, "Now I've got it." Don't neglect the gift, but stir it up, as Scripture says in I Timothy 1:6 – 7. When you don't know exactly how to pray about a situation, or you just feel unable to pray effectively, pray in tongues. It bypasses the intellect, and your spirit will be praying through you. That's part of casting our care on Him.

Be blessed, emboldened, and encouraged to receive the power of the Holy Spirit. He opens your understanding and gives you revelation and insight into Scripture and things He has for your life. I believe the humbling and yielding of our tongue is a doorway into an exciting walk with God for the rest of your life! The Holy Spirit wants to be your Friend and have fellowship with you, give you comfort and guidance, peace, and joy, daily!

Printed in the United States
by Baker & Taylor Publisher Services